Classroom Management

Classroom Management

A Case Study Handbook for Teachers of Challenging Learners

Allan G. Osborne, Jr.
Assistant Principal,
Snug Harbor Community School
Quincy, Massachusetts
Visiting Associate Professor,
Bridgewater State College

Philip A. DiMattia
Adjunct Associate Professor,
Boston College
Director, Boston College Campus School

Carolina Academic Press
Durham, North Carolina

Library of Congress Cataloging-in-Publication Data

Osborne, Allan G.
    Classroom management : a case study handbook for teachers of
challenging learners / Allan G. Osborne, Jr., Philip DiMattia
        p.   cm.
    Includes bibliographical references (p.) and index.
    ISBN 0-89089-873-1 (paper)
    1. Classroom management—Handbooks, manuals, etc.
2. Problem children—Education—Handbooks, manuals, etc.
I. DiMattia, Philip. II. Title.
LB30313.075 1998
371.102'4—dc21   98-6539
                                                                     CIP

CAROLINA ACADEMIC PRESS
700 Kent Street
Durham, North Carolina 27701
Telephone (919) 489-7486
Facsimile (919) 493-5668
www.cap-press.com

Printed in the United States of America.

To Debbie and Gerry

Contents

Preface

Every classroom needs discipline and order. Without it the students cannot learn. It is hoped, however, that the teacher can apply the classroom rules with a concern for the individual student. This concern for the individual can lead to a discovery of why an individual child misbehaves. A concern for the individual may also lead to a solution to the problem.

A personal disciplinary system that centers on concern for the individual students also leads to discipline with respect. When discipline must be administered, both the student and the teacher should be able to leave the situation with self-respect. If either the teacher or the student leaves the situation with a loss of self-respect, future encounters can only be negative and the long-term prospect of solving the student's behavioral problems is reduced.

This text was written to address a need for a classroom management case studies book designed to improve the skills of current and prospective classroom teachers. The authors hope that this case book will help to prepare teachers for inclusive classrooms containing great learner diversity. As we approach the 21st century, this learner diversity is expected to increase.

This project was an outgrowth of professional development activities for experienced and beginning teachers at the graduate level. The themes included in the manuscript are based on a needs assessment conducted over a four year period on two college campuses with over 200 teachers participating. The needs assessment indicated that teachers wanted an experiential text that would assist them in developing an ongoing system of classroom discipline responsive to the human conditions their students experience. Sarason has suggested that if teachers ignore or are insensitive to the questions, feelings, attitudes and strivings of students, then those whom they seek to influence will respond with resistance (either overt or covert), apathy and passivity.[1] This text is intended to help teachers provide a human response to a human need by better understanding the underlying causes of behavior.

This text is designed to provide the classroom teacher with practical applications and exercises on dealing effectively with the consequences of

---

1. Sarason, S. (1993). *The Case of Change: Rethinking the Preparation of Educators.* Thousand Oaks, CA: Corwin Press.

conflict that arise in classroom settings, both within individuals and groups, as a natural result of adult and child expectations of each other. In this way the nature of conflict can be viewed in a contextual and developmental perspective; leading to a greater understanding of why teachers and students are together in the first place. This text is based on the philosophy that teachers and students are far more effective if classroom management is perceived, not as an issue of control, but as an issue of helping individuals grow positively by learning new habits of thinking and practice.[2]

Recent calls for educational reform have dramatically challenged conventional wisdom and the fundamental principles underlying the prevalent knowledge base in general education. Reform advocates in teacher education have called for the recognition that teaching is active as opposed to passive, and learning is developmental and contextual as opposed to static and sterile. Sarason has emphasized that the single most important factor for determining successful reform is teacher recognition that their professional training needs must focus on the understanding of the current circumstances of students.[3] Otherwise teaching will not be driven by a response to student developmental needs that is essential to bring about substantial and lasting reform.

Diverse learners in general classroom settings are becoming more and more commonplace with increasing universal access to school by all children. Classroom teachers, administrators, curriculum supervisors, parents and public policy makers are often at a loss as to how to plan for and manage this expanding reality. This text will guide teachers in their ongoing professional development of habits of reflective classroom management practices that promote individual and group development consistent with best practice research. As a case book it will serve as a resource for analyzing some of the unique situations that often arise in typical classrooms. It is designed to fortify teachers to be better prepared when they encounter deeply complex and challenging behaviors from others. A fundamental rationale is that in interpersonal interactions involving persons of all ages, individuals not only screen the environment they find themselves in, but also influence the way other individuals respond to them.

This is a book about conflict and how to use it to build positive development. The case method of instruction was chosen as it promotes a dialectic mode of inquiry that requires active participation and dialogue. This methodology recognizes that the single most important factor for learn-

---

2. Jones, V. & Jones, L. (1990). *Comprehensive Classroom Management*. Boston: Allyn & Bacon.

3. Sarason, S. (1993). *The Case of Change: Rethinking the Preparation of Teachers*. Thousand Oaks, CA: Corwin Press.

ing is the individual intellect itself, guided by the knowledge base of best practice and current research on human development.

Much of the material that is included in this book has already been successfully used in staff development programs and graduate course work. The material is designed to offer practical applications derived from theoretical grounding. Using a case study method of instruction allows participants to develop habits of reflective practice. Techniques include use of experiential simulations, examination and analysis of situations, and refinement of practices. The case material will allow teachers to gain greater insight into the contextual relationships among various factors present in a classroom, including stress, anxiety, defiance, untruthfulness, cheating, stealing, and the physical, emotional, social, and moral development of students. Through the use of these case materials, which are based on the authors' own experiences as classroom teachers and administrators, teachers will develop diagnostic and predictive skills that will enable them to change student behaviors that impede successful learning.

Chapters are organized around themes that reflect the typical causes of behavior disorders in children. Each chapter begins with a brief overview of the disorder as manifested in a classroom situation. A bibliography of sources for additional reading is included after the brief introductory comments. Selections from the bibliography will provide the reader with additional information on the etiology of and effective classroom strategies for dealing with the behavior disorder that is the subject of the chapter. Each chapter contains five classroom scenarios or case studies with questions for reflection and discussion. This book is not designed to be a comprehensive text on behavioral interventions. Several excellent texts currently exist on this topic. Rather, this book is designed to be used as supplemental material in conjunction with any one of the available texts.

The exercises provided in this book will contribute to the development of higher order thinking and analytical practices. They will provide teachers with a means for practical application of specific methodologies and strategies that can be used to develop habits of reflective practice in their students. These practical applications will provide the teachers with the tools necessary to successfully manage student behavior in a variety of situations and settings. The insight gained from the case studies in this text will result in improved problem-solving and decision-making skills.

Use of case study procedures permits the reader to examine a slice of behavior to construct meaning that the practitioner can build upon over time. This will bring about improved understanding of the specific conditions under which individuals labor and struggle. Each chapter includes exercises that suggest plausible predictions that require various human resource elements for furthering of discussion and practice. The factors that make up the learning environment are thus seen as panoramic in a context that oftentimes needs assistance to understand. Throughout the work the central focus is on individual student development and the teacher's responsibility to create appropriate positive settings that encourage growth.

As indicated above, the book includes numerous exercises and sample cases that will assist teachers in refining collaborative and consultational skills for working with school-wide assistance teams, school-based assistance teams, teacher assistance teams, and child study teams to better understand complex problems. The self-reflective exercises that accompany each case study encourage teachers to judge their own comfort level with increasingly more challenging behaviors. This material provides scenarios of behavioral misconduct incidents that typically occur in classrooms today. The case studies range from vignettes of mild to severe problems. Students profiled in these case studies represent various age levels, social positions, and educational levels. Each case study is followed by a set of questions for reflection and discussion. This material is designed so that professors or staff development leaders can choose which case studies would be most appropriate for their respective clientele. Although the reflective questions provided for each case study are designed to lead the reader to logical conclusions, no "right" answers to the study questions are provided. This is to allow for the development of personal classroom management strategies that reflect the skills and personalities of individual practitioners. Furthermore, it is felt that not providing a set of right or even probable strategies for dealing with the behavior contained in the case studies will allow the instructor greater freedom and flexibility in terms of leading group discussions.

Since the disciplinary process is very much a legal process with numerous requirements that must be carried out properly, a brief discussion of legal requirements is included in Appendix A. This is designed to only provide a summary overview of the legal requirements. The reader who is unfamiliar with the legal issues surrounding discipline is advised to consult any one of many textbooks on school law.

As indicated above, the case studies in this book are designed to elicit reflective responses from both in-service and pre-service teachers. Instructors are, of course, free to use them as they see fit. It is suggested, however, that the questions following each case study be used to generate discussion with the ultimate task being to develop a long range behavior interaction plan for the student. The instructor interested in additional resources on how to use the case study method is referred to Appendix B.

A word on how the case studies are organized into chapters may be in order. The ten chapters were developed to identify the most common types of misbehavior found in classrooms today. Case studies were then chosen that illustrated each type of behavior. All of these case studies are based on actual situations. Although certain details have been altered to protect the identities of the students and teachers, the presentation of the behavioral problems remains factual. Since students who have behavioral problems generally exhibit more than one type of misconduct, it was difficult to determine in which chapters many of these case studies best fit. The authors tried to place each case study into the chapter that was concerned with the predominant behavior exhibited by the student. The reader is asked to understand that human behavior is complex and does not neatly fall into discrete categories. A decision was made by the authors to not alter the facts in the case studies to make them better fit the chapters in which they were included.

It would not be possible to undertake a project such as this without the support and encouragement of many friends, relatives, and colleagues. First, we wish to acknowledge the contributions of our graduate students in helping us to choose appropriate case studies for inclusion in this book. All of the material in the book has been field tested on our graduate students who have made numerous suggestions that were incorporated into the final draft. We also wish to thank our professional associates for critically reviewing the material and making many suggestions for improvement. Finally, our families have been extremely supportive and understanding when we needed to take time away from them to work on the many drafts of this manuscript. Special thanks in this regard goes to our wives, Debbie and Gerry, who are still patiently waiting for us to write that million dollar best seller.

Classroom Management

Chapter 1

Conduct Disorders with Aggressive Overtones: The Bully

During the drive home Ms. Vaz found herself unusually preoccupied with thoughts about the day's events in her second grade classroom. "Jamie was really so unkind with ethnic name calling. Monica was hurt and confused. She and Jamie have gotten along so well in the past. During recess, all Jamie did was fight with his peers over turns at bat. I know he knows the rules, but, his outbursts are so intimidating to other kids. He has no idea how that alienates him from his peers. Come to think of it Jamie was out of control most of the day. At lunch there was that food business with Tony. I still don't know who started throwing food first. Why did he have to throw food at the others? They are so threatened by his bullying, they are timid and vulnerable. I was trying to convince Maria to eat so that she would feel better and I did not see what was going on between Jamie and Tony. What you don't see you really can not judge fairly. It is just not always possible to be with it when you are alone in a classroom with twenty-eight seven-year-old children. The afternoon wasn't much better for Jamie, with the outburst in the activity group. He could have really seriously injured Matt with his pencil! I have to remember to make certain that my kids use dull pencil tips. That was really scary the more I think of it. What explains all this oppositional behavior?"

Her thoughts continued. "I know for so many of my kids these are rough times, with so many mothers needing to work, so many kids without fathers, little to no extended family nearby, single parents who have so many recidivistic relationships that move in and out of these kids lives. These have got to take their toll on them! Don't others see the consequences? Well you would never know it to look at school board agendas!"

"I am really beginning to get weary of it all. Some days I feel like I just can't take it any longer. I can feel a growing anger that is disturbing and a little frightening at the same time. If I'm not there for them — who will be? These kids don't stand a chance without some stability and predictability for some parts of their day. I want so much for them to experience success in school so they can feel valued and important. But still, it just doesn't seem fair that I should feel the need to play so many different roles, especially those for which I don't feel very skilled. While I am feeling my own

3

rage building, the truth is, I am getting scared. I have never felt this way about teaching before. Is what I worked so hard to achieve going to end up being something that I fail at? All I ever wanted to be was a teacher."

"Jamie's behavior really shattered my personal confidence today. I was not in total charge and that's frightening, Jamie behaved like a real bully and I was not effective dealing with such behavior. How long can I continue as a teacher? It is so much of a challenge today. How many people really understand that. I wonder! Now I'm mad at the whole world. Oh, Lord help me!

There is a good chance that most if not all teachers at some point think about the events in their classrooms. Whatever their personal approach in the way they conduct this internal dialogue, it has many benefits. One of the major benefits of such retrospective thinking is that it can provide a means for acquiring insight into what took place today to become more fortified in facing tomorrow. It also helps to recognize one's own limitations to avoid repeating mistakes at a later time.

What may be important here is that through such a process, teachers are able to hone diagnostic and other problem solving skills. While this may sound somewhat academic it is also a very practical behavior to acquire. The next day is surely going to come and bring surprises with it. After all, one of the great challenges of teaching is the spontaneity that students possess that influences their expressive behaviors. Teachers, like Ms. Vaz, want to make such a difference that all students are able to achieve school success. They are expected to respond to many diverse forms of classroom issues that challenge their problem solving capacities.

Students who present conduct problems with aggressive features present highly special issues and problems that need attention. The action a teacher takes in these situations gives meaning and direction to such behaviors and influences their effect on others. Sometimes there are life long consequences. Understanding problem behavior presents a significant challenge to teachers on a regular basis. While frequency, duration and intensity, as well as chronicity, are observable factors that help to determine severity, it is the emotional immaturity of such forms of behavior that constrain the internal adaptive capacity of the student to adjust social behavior with regularity. Loss of control issues, along with emotional immaturity, are interrelated as part of the same problem; yet often are poorly understood and accepted as part of the classroom teacher's challenge and responsibility.

In the example above, note the direction of the behaviors manifested by Jamie. They tend to move away from Jamie and are directed toward other individuals. The behaviors are aimed at invading other individuals' personal space and serve to evoke some degree of retaliation from peers or the teacher. One result of reaction is to make it extremely difficult to achieve an immediate and meaningful resolution that permits each actor some degree of satisfaction and a sense of personal justice. Often, teachers must settle for an imperfect resolution without knowing what price each student in the classroom pays for the reaction by the teacher. This becomes especially significant if there is any truth to the statement, "What is happening to students while they are learning is far more important then what they learn." A teacher's understanding of the hidden curriculum factors of crowds, power, and praise and their influence on the social development of students is critical to understanding the effects of conduct problems. One of the important aspects of Jamie's behavior toward others in the example is the selectivity of whom he victimizes. They are weaker, more vulnerable, and unlikely to prevail in opposing his assaults.

Bullying is just one of the behaviors associated with conduct problems that teachers find complicated and difficult to correct within a large general education classroom. Other behaviors that are associated with conduct problems include: lying, stealing, fighting, cursing, cheating, disrespect for and destroying property. These are also behaviors that can be described as moving against others or invading the personal space of others. Each serves to evoke some degree of response. If the kind of response is retaliatory by peers or by adults, escalation rather than resolution takes place. These behaviors differ from bullying behavior primarily in the selectivity of victims. These behaviors have been identified in research by Achenbach and Edelbrock that they referred to as externalizing, and under-controlled factors.[1]

What is common however, to all of these behaviors is that they represent limit setting issues. They include impulsivity and poor judgment that significantly impair internal adaptive controls. To specifically understand bullying behavior, it is necessary to examine the constraints upon internal adaptive mechanisms and the relationship of the expectations that exist between and among participants.

Limit setting represents a universal problem for both children and adults. Think of the excesses that each of us struggle with to bring under control. For some it is food, alcohol, poor judgments in relationships, unnecessary purchases, excessive work. For others it may be postponement of adolescence. Whatever the excess there is a constant struggle within each person to bring a balance to the major life priorities that bring about a calm and peaceful existence. At this moment Jamie's teacher is struggling with two

1. Achenbach, T.M. (1985). *Assessment and Taxonomy of Child and Adolescent Psychopathology.* Beverly Hills, CA: Sage. Achenbach, T.M. and Edelbrock, C.S. (1984). *Child Behavior Checklist: Teacher's Report.* Burlington, VT: University Associates in Psychiatry. Achenbach, T.M. and Edelbrock, C.S. (1989). Diagnostic, taxonomic, and assessment issues. In T.H. Ollendick & M. Hersen (Eds.) *Handbook of Child Psychopathology.* New York: Plenum.

aspects of limit setting. First, how to deal with her personal commitment as a teacher. Is it time to limit her longevity? The other limit setting issue is one she will have to face the next morning, when she greets her second graders. How will she handle that?

Limit setting skills result from a person's increased experience in dealing with stress, stressors and delaying the need for immediate satisfaction. From adults this is expected, it is presumed that they have developed and matured. For children, however, this is a goal to be achieved over time and with much teaching of appropriate social behavior. When young children come to school having been exposed to some early development of social adaptation skills, the ongoing development in this area is more routine, natural, and reenforced through experiences with peers. But, what about those children who do not have the same positive early experiences for a variety of reasons? They present an additional responsibility for the classroom teacher who will need to include the teaching of social skill behaviors as part of the total curriculum.

When children have flawed internal adaptive mechanisms that prevent adequate adaptations to what are otherwise appropriate expectations from legitimate adults, then conduct problems that move against others can increase in direct proportion to the limit setting expectations that are requested. It is within the relationship of the teacher's expectations and student limit setting stage of development that problems arise that require careful examination of the what, why, when and how. Thus, practices in the classroom can be adjusted to provide effective responses so that all students can achieve and experience high levels of learning and behavior competence. The challenge for Ms. Vaz tomorrow is to reaffirm her commitment to create a learning atmosphere of protective caring, sufficient enough to reduce anxiety in each student to encourage growth in both adaptive and academic behaviors. Her first task will be to engage Jamie in a work experience for positive change in his behavior. The eyes of every other student will be watching. The professional limit setting issue for Ms. Vaz will be vastly influenced by her results.

There are a number of strategies that the teacher can draw upon to begin her challenge. First, and most vital, is a focus on getting Jamie's attention to begin a win-win resolution process. Is this a situation where the long talk might be a starting point? What about teacher supervision and physical proximity positioning during various activities? Would rethinking of classroom groups allow for Jamie to be with more formidable peers?

Since each circumstance is unique, problems of bullying must be handled case by case. Some will respond to the restructuring that can take place in the classroom whereby the teacher provides the necessary leadership and support so that all students feel safe and secure, physically and emotionally. Every student has a right to his/her own personal safe space to learn. Other situations on the other hand, will require the extensive services of ancillary specialists through the resources commonly available to the school district such as; school counselors, special education professionals, school psychologists, and mental health professionals in the community. If parents are included early on in any effort to change bullying behavior, chances of success are greatly increased. Teachers should be fortified against becoming discouraged with the involvement of parents in the beginning who may be somewhat resistant or defensive in conversation about their child. The involvement of other professionals will blunt any negative impact. Once parents become comfortable with school professionals whom they come to recognize as positive allies, their resistance will disappear.

Additional Reading

Achenbach, T.M. (1985). *Assessment and Taxonomy of Child and Adolescent Psychopathology.* Beverly Hills, CA: Sage.

Achenbach, T. M., and Edelbrock, C. S. (1984). *Child Behavior Checklist: Teacher's Report.* Burlington, VT: University Associates in Psychiatry.

Achenbach, T. M., and Edelbrock, C. S. (1989). Diagnostic, taxonomic, and assessment issues. In T. H. Ollendick and M. Hersen (Eds.), *Handbook of Child Psychopathology* (2nd ed.). New York: Plenum.

Bandura, A. (1973). *Aggression: A Social Learning Analysis.* Englewood Cliffs, NJ: Prentice-Hall.

Baragar, J. (1992). A counselor's concept of time off for "bad behavior." *Guidance and Counseling, 8(2).*

Batsche, G., and Knoff, H. (1994). Bullies and their victims: Understanding a pervasive problem in schools. *School Psychology Review, 23(2),* 165–174.

Byrne, B. (1994). *Coping with Bullying in Schools.* London, England: Cassell Publishers.

Cole, P.M., Zahn-Waxler, C., and Smith, K.D. (1994). Expressive control during a disappointment: Variations related to preschoolers' behavior problems. *Developmental Psychology, 30,* 835–46.

Kauffman, J. M. (1994). Taming aggression in the young: A call to action. *Education Week (March 16), 13(25),* 43.

Long, N. J., Morse, W. C., and Newman, R. G. (Eds.). (1965). *Conflict in the Classroom.* Belmont, CA: Wadsworth.

Morse, W. C. (1965). Intervention techniques for the classroom teacher. In P. Knoblock (Ed.), *Educational Programming for Emotionally Disturbed Children: The Decade Ahead.* Syracuse, NY: Syracuse University Press.

Olweus, D. (1995). Peer abuse or bullying at school: Basic facts and a school-based intervention programme. *Prospects*, March.

Quay, H.C. (1986). Conduct disorders. In H.C. Quay and J.S. Werry (Eds.), *Psychopathological Disorders of Childhood* (3rd ed.). New York: Wiley.

Quay, H.C., and Peterson, D.R. (1987). *Manual for the Revised Behavior Problem Checklist*. Coral Gables, FL: Author.

Redl, F. (1959). The concept of a therapeutic milieu. *American Journal of Orthopsychiatry, 29*, 721–734.

Redl, F. (1959). The concept of life space interview. *American Journal of Orthopsychiatry, 29*, 1–18.

Redl, F. (1966). Designing a therapeutic classroom environment for disturbed children: The Milieu approach. In P. Knoblock (Ed.), *Intervention Approaches in Educating Emotionally Disturbed Children*. Syracuse, NY: Syracuse University Press.

Rhodes, W. C. (1967). The disturbing Child: A problem of ecological management. *Exceptional Children, 33*, 449–455.

Case Studies

Case Study #1-1

Student: Willy

Background: Willy is a 7 year old first grader attending a parochial school. There are 25 students in his classroom. Willy receives Title I services for reading in school and private psychotherapy. He attended kindergarten in the public schools and at the end of the year it was recommended that he repeat the year. Instead, however, his father enrolled him in the parochial school where he did repeat the first grade. Willy is the youngest of seven children. His parents are divorced and his father has custody of all seven children. His mother, who is an alcoholic, rarely visits him. Willy's father is quite well off financially and has hired domestic help to see to the children's needs. Due to the nature of his job he works long hours and frequently works on week-ends.

Willy has a poor attention span and has difficulty finishing assignments unless he is receiving one-on-one attention. More significantly, however, he is very aggressive toward his peers. He is prone to angry outbursts and will strike out physically when angered. Often, when he is unhappy with a situation, he throws a temper tantrum. His teacher has tried several behavior modification techniques such as stickers and charts to no avail. However, she has not been trained in behavior modification and is not sure she is properly implementing the strategies. She knows that she is not as consistent as she should be; but with 25 students it is difficult to find the time to provide Willy with immediate feedback.

Presenting problem: Willy's behavior is worsening. The school's principal is not supportive. He had previously refused to set up a conference with Willy's father because he didn't want to alienate Mr. Makit. Mr. Makit has made large financial contributions to the school in the past.

The problem reached a boiling point recently when Willy threw a pair of scissors at another student. When the parents of the other student demanded that something be done about "this bully," the principal finally contacted Mr. Makit. A conference was held and it was recommended that Mr. Makit contact the public schools to have Willy evaluated. It was suggested that he might be a candidate for a public school program for students with behavioral disorders. Mr. Makit refused because he wants Willy to have a religious education. Instead he offered to pay for a classroom aide if the parochial school would allow Willy to stay. The principal readily agreed.

Questions for reflection and discussion:

1. What factors, or life experiences may have contributed to Willy's aggressive behavior?
2. Willy's teacher, by her own admission, is not well versed in behavior modification or other behavior intervention strategies. What additional training would help her better meet Willy's needs?
3. How can Willy's teacher best utilize the services of the aide? What should the aide do to help control Willy's behavior? Should the aide be given any specific training?
4. Willy is already receiving psychotherapy. What other services would be beneficial?
5. Should Willy be placed in a special education classroom or can he be educated in the parochial school, as his father desires, without causing harm to other students?

Case Study #1-2

Student: Sally

Background: Sally is a 4-year old kindergarten student. She has one older brother and one younger sister. Her father is a dentist and her mother is an attorney. She has been diagnosed as having a conduct disorder and a multiple personality disorder. At home she has been known to abuse family pets and throw temper tantrums when she doesn't get her own way. Neither of her siblings has demonstrated any behavioral aberrations. Sally attended a special education pre-school program and is receiving play therapy. She was placed in the regular education kindergarten pursuant to the school district's inclusion policy.

In her kindergarten class she has difficulty waiting her turn in play activities and can strike out at other children without provocation. She has physically attacked other students in the form of biting, choking, and kicking. Following these incidents she had told a counselor that a magic butterfly told her to hurt the other children. As a result of her aggressive tendencies, she does not have any friends. She is currently attending an all day kindergarten class. There are only 15 students in the class and the class has a paraprofessional in addition to the teacher.

Presenting problem: Sally refused to sit at a table with other children because boys were at the table. When told to sit at the table Sally stated, "Boys are ugly, I don't like them." When she was prodded to sit at the table she started screaming, threw a box of crayons at the paraprofessional, knocked over a chair, tore up another child's art work, and physically lashed out at anyone who came near her. During this time she alternately screamed and growled. Sally had to be put in a four-point restraint and was totally isolated from the class for the remainder of the day.

Since that incident other students are afraid of Sally. Several parents are demanding that either Sally be taken out of the class or else they are going to remove their own children from the school. One has even threatened to sue the school district if Sally is not removed from the class. Sally's parents, on the other hand, are adamant that she remain where she is, feeling that she will benefit most from a placement in which she has positive role models.

Questions for reflection and discussion:

1. Is a regular kindergarten class the proper placement for a student diagnosed as having a conduct disorder and multiple personalities?
2. Besides the paraprofessional, what other supplementary aides and services could be provided to allow Sally to be educated in an inclusionary setting?
3. Does Sally require more than just play therapy? What other types of psychological intervention services would be appropriate for a 4 ½ year old child?
4. How can school officials respond to the parents of the other students who are demanding Sally's removal?
5. Are Sally's parents correct that she will benefit from exposure to positive role models in the form of the other students in the class? How can

Sally's need for positive role models be reconciled with the safety needs of the other students?

Case Study #1-3

Student: Michael

Background: Michael is a bright, but arrogant, eleventh grade student. He tends to be insensitive to other students and often tries to intimidate them. He is physically larger and stronger than his peers and frequently uses his physical abilities to bully the other students. Academically, Michael is at the top of his class and seems motivated to excel scholastically. However, his general classroom and school behavior is entirely another matter. Michael tends to be very loud and boisterous. Between classes he charges through the hallways with little regard for whether or not he hurts someone. If he knocks another student over, he won't even stop to see if the student is hurt. He also shows little regard for the property of others.

Michael's mother is on the school board and those who have met her clearly understand where Michael gets his arrogance. She is in the school on a regular basis as a volunteer. Otherwise she is not employed. Michael's father is an executive in a large local company that makes many equipment and monetary donations to the school. School personnel have had very few dealings with the father as he works long hours and travels frequently. Michael generally has the best of everything.

The school Michael attends is known for excellence, having been the recipient of many honors, including the federal Department of Education's "Blue Ribbon School" award. Most of its students go on to college. Over 90% of the students attending the school come from affluent families who put much pressure on the faculty to make sure their children excel.

Presenting problem: Michael's classroom behavior was getting even worse by the day. Two major concerns were that he openly made fun of less academically-able students, and he spoke to his teachers in a very disrespectful manner. When teachers spoke to him about his behavior, he mockingly told them to mind their own business. He also told them that they better not cross him or else his father would cut off the donations and his mother would see to it that they were on the unemployment line. Most teachers, having encountered his mother, were intimidated by his comments.

Things came to a head one day when Michael grabbed a tape recorder off a blind student's desk and threw it out an open window. His excuse was that the sound of the tape hissing was distracting him. The school's principal reluctantly scheduled a suspension hearing, partly due to threats from the blind student's parents that they would file a discrimination lawsuit if disciplinary action was not taken. Michael's mother was not at all supportive. She stated that the incident never would have happened if Michael had not been seated near the blind student, "where his equipment naturally would be distracting."

Michael's mother also made several statements indicating that she resented the amount of money the school district was required to spend educating its disabled students. She further indicated that it would make much more sense to spend those funds on bright students like Michael. "After all," she mused, "They're the future business leaders of this country."

Michael was given a one day suspension. His mother immediately appealed to the superintendent. In her appeal she stated that the punishment was unjust for someone who was a model student.

Questions for reflection and discussion:

1. Why does Michael feel the need to intimidate and bully other students? Can his actions toward his teachers also be classified as bullying?
2. How does Michael's mother's response (and her own attitudes) feed into his bullying behavior?
3. It appears that school staff may not have kept Michael's mother fully informed of his past behavior. How has this come back to haunt them?
4. How can the faculty effectively deal with Michael in the future? How can they deal with his mother?
5. If the superintendent reverses the suspension, what should be the staff's response to Michael?

Case Study #1-4

Student: Earl

Background: Earl is a 10 year old fifth grader. He is the youngest child in an intact family of five children, three boys and two girls. An 11 year old male cousin also lives with the family. Earl's father is employed by the city's Department of Public Works. His mother is not employed but is currently in a job training program. The family lives in subsidized housing.

Earl is rather large for his age and is very aggressive. He enjoys sports but has a tendency to try to be the "hero" rather than a team player. He also seems to have a must win at all costs attitude. He has difficulty following the rules of the game, is often accused of cheating, and just as often accuses others of cheating. When accused of cheating, he becomes enraged and, if an adult supervisor is not around, will make physical threats against the accuser. He frequently threatens other students with, "I'll get you after school." Since Earl is larger than most of his peers, he is able to dominate them physically. Most will simply back off and let him have his own way.

Another problem Earl has is that he is not very honest. Even in the face of overwhelming evidence he will deny wrongdoing. For example, when he is caught bullying other students, he will respond by accusing them of starting it. Even when an adult staff member has witnessed the entire confrontation, Earl will insist that the other student started the fight by either striking at him first or calling him names. One of his favorite claims is that "he said something about my mother." To make matters worse, Earl's mother generally believes his side of the story and becomes very defensive when called in for a disciplinary conference. She has accused the principal of never believing anything Earl says and of not being fair when dealing with Earl.

Presenting problem: Recently Earl has been involved in two incidents of theft. In the first incident his teacher returned to her classroom early following lunch and found Earl and another boy, Jimmy, in the classroom. Earl had one candy bar in his hand and another in his pocket. Jimmy did not have any candy bars in his possession. The candy bars had come from the teacher's closet. Jimmy admitted that they had stolen the candy bars but insisted that it had been Earl's idea. He said he knew it was wrong, but was afraid to not go along with Earl's plan. Jimmy also stated that Earl frequently stole candy bars and other snacks from other students. Earl, on the other hand, claimed that Jimmy had stolen the candy bars and that he had taken them away to return them to the teacher. Each boy was given a one day in-school suspension. Earl's mother appealed the suspension to the assistant superintendent who upheld the disciplinary action.

The second incident involved the theft of a basketball shirt from another student. The school offered an intramural basketball program but had a policy that you couldn't play if you didn't bring your team shirt. During one game the referee noticed that Earl had his shirt on inside out. He told Earl to change the shirt so that his number was showing. Earl said that he was wearing the shirt inside out because it was dirty. The referee told him that he couldn't play if his number wasn't showing. When Earl reversed the shirt, it was discovered that the shirt did not have his number on it. It turned out that he had taken the shirt from another player's locker. That player was aware that Earl had taken the shirt from his locker, but again, was afraid to say anything for fear of reprisal. Once again, Earl denied that he had taken the shirt, but rather, insisted that he had found it in his locker and didn't realize that it wasn't his shirt. A suspension hearing was held at which Earl's mother vehemently defended her son and threatened to sue if he was given a suspension. The principal stood firm and issued a two day suspension.

Questions for reflection and discussion:

1. Why does Earl feel the need to dominate and bully other students? Is his must win at all costs attitude related to his need to dominate?
2. Are the stealing incidents related to the bullying incidents? Does this represent different manifestations of the same problem? Is stealing an act of aggression?
3. How is Earl's mother's behavior fueling the fire? What can school officials do to get her to be more cooperative? If they are unable to win her over as an ally, how can they counteract her negative attitude?
4. The fact that other students are afraid to speak up when Earl wrongs them is also a serious problem. How can school officials effectively deal with this.
5. What long-range strategies can the staff employ to deal with Earl's aggressive behavior?

Case Study #1-5

Student: Omari

Background: Omari is fourteen years old and attending the eighth grade of a middle school in a large urban community. He has been in foster care since he was three months old. His mother was thirteen years old when she became pregnant by an older man who was already married with children of his own. He disclaimed both Omari and his mother at birth and has consistently resisted any attempts to become involved with his alleged son. Omari's mother was unable to care for him after his birth so he was placed in the custody of the state department of child services. For the past six years Omari has been with the same foster parents who wish to adopt him. However, they think it is best that they wait until he is older so that he can be more certain that he wishes to have them as parents. Omari has always liked school and is well motivated academically. For the past two years however, teachers noticed that his behavior has changed. While he still is doing well academically, his social behaviors are becoming increasingly problematic. He has no friends among his peers, and, in fact, they tend to avoid and ignore him. When teachers have tried to inquire why this is so, they are generally told that Omari bullies them, uses suggestive language with the girls in the group, and is difficult to get along with unless he has his own way. He scares the other students with stories that his real father is a drug dealer from whom he steals and sells drugs on the street after school. Recently, teachers began to pay more attention in individual classrooms to see if they could identify what might be going on.

Presenting problem: Omari's teachers decided that it would be useful to observe him in different school settings during the day. They agreed to be especially alert to his behavior outside of the classroom. When they began to compare notes a somewhat different description of Omari began to emerge. It was observed that behaviors that were thought to take place outside the classroom were being displayed inside as well. Omari was having more and more difficulty functioning in large groups. His female teachers reported that he frequently would wander around the room with his work effort and quality suffering, that he was displaying immature behaviors more, and doing things that disrupted his peers. On a number of occasions they described his wandering as aimless while at other times his wandering was focused, whereby he would walk over to a peer and throw something or take the peer's things and hide them. It seemed that his interactions were based on bothering people. The difficulty these teachers had with Omari was that he denied ever doing these actions even when he was seen doing them. His standard response was "It's not me" even when he was caught doing the action. Because of these instances, female teachers feel that they can not trust his words or his actions. To add to the lack of trust, it has been reported that he has stolen things from both the school and his foster parents. When spoken to about anything that he might have done wrong, his response has been, "I could give a care." It is interesting to note that his male teachers have not experienced the same issues with Omari. While he does stay by himself a lot, and remains aloof, he has not presented similar problems in their classes. While teachers are at a loss to explain Omari's behavior, there is concern about his disregard for his peers and their right to be free to learn.

Questions for discussion and reflection:

1. What are some issues that should be explored to understand the needs of this student?
2. What kind of interventions are indicated to help Omari give up the inappropriate classroom behaviors that he exhibits?
3. Is there evidence that may suggest that Omari does not know how to make friends among his peers? If this is so, what actions would you suggest the teacher undertake?
4. What might explain the difference between Omari's behavior with female and male teachers?
5. Do you think that counseling would help Omari deal with his birth circumstances? Why or why not?
6. Would you recommend some assistance for the foster parent as a way to help determine when would be an appropriate time for Omari to decide on adoption?

Chapter 2

Issues of Power: A Tug of War

Mrs. Liscombe couldn't believe she had done it again. She had allowed Mike to engage her in a power struggle once more. And worse yet, once again, Mike had won!

Mrs. King, the guidance counselor had warned her about this. Mike was only nine years old, but he seemed to take great pleasure in being involved in confrontations with adults. Mike was a bright child, but he was very manipulative. He seemed accustomed to getting his own way.

Today's episode began when Mike refused to put the software he had been using away. He stated that he hadn't taken it out so he didn't see why he had to put it away. Mrs. Liscombe had explained that although he wasn't the one who had taken it out, he was the last one to have used it and therefore should be the one to put it away. Mike was adamant that he wasn't going to put the software away. Mrs. Liscombe was just as adamant that he was! A battle of words and actions escalated until it reached the point where Mrs. Liscombe had to call the vice principal. Although Mike spent some time in the office and missed a recess, the bottom line was that he didn't put the software away.

As the guidance counselor had pointed out so many times, in Mike's mind he had won the confrontation. Worse still, he viewed Mrs. Liscombe as someone who didn't have authority over him because she always had to call for help when they had these confrontations. She knew she shouldn't let these confrontations even begin, let alone escalate; but what was she to do when Mike refused to do as he was told?

In an ideal classroom situation the teacher is the boss and no student would ever question the teacher's authority. In the real world such classrooms rarely, if ever, exist. The fact is that many students question the teacher's authority and some outright defy it. If a teacher is not able to effectively deal with challenges to his or her authority, chaos will soon result. That is not to say that a classroom cannot be run in a democratic manner. There is a big difference between allowing students to participate in decision-making and allowing one or more students to disrupt the classroom with their constant defiant, challenging behavior. These students frequently argue or contradict the teacher and may even throw tantrums when they do not get their own way.

The issue comes down to the difference between power and control. Effective teachers are able to maintain control without necessarily using power. By structuring their classrooms so that the interests and needs of all students can be met, these teachers are able to maintain well-disciplined classrooms. Conflict is inevitable in today's classroom. How effectively the teacher is able to manage conflict and engage students in self-management of their own behavior may be the difference between chaos and order.

Some students have difficulty taking direction from anyone. They resent being told what to do. They do not respect, let alone obey, any adult authority figures in their lives, whether it be a parent, a teacher, a principal, a scout leader, or a police officer. These students may express the opinion that it's a "free country" and they can do what they want when they want. Other students respect (or fear) the authority of certain people, such as their parents, but do not view other adults, such as teachers, as having authority over them. Still others may recognize the authority of some teachers but not others. Students who openly defy the authority of the teacher are among the most difficult to deal with in a classroom situation.

Teachers frequently engage in a tug of war with defiant students, struggling to see who will eventually win the power struggle. Unfortunately this is usually a no win situation for both. When the teacher maintains a "must win at all costs" attitude, the student usually ends up being subjected to serious disciplinary sanctions. However, the problem is not resolved. Following the disciplinary action the student remains defiant and the teacher remains stressed. In fact, the student's misbehavior is actually reinforced because the student succeeded in engaging in a confrontation with the teacher. Most likely the student's primary goal *was* to engage the teacher in a confrontation. Thus, when a teacher engages in a tug of war with a student, the student has achieved the goal.

One pitfall to avoid is backing this student into a corner. Generally a power-seeking student will come out fighting. A student who is initially defensive may take the offensive if backed into a corner. It is important for the teacher to understand that maintaining control of the classroom requires more than just dominance. Engaging in a power struggle with the student is counter-productive. If the behavior cannot be ignored it is best to acknowledge the student's need for attention and even acknowledge that the student has the ability to disrupt the classroom. Naturally, if the student becomes violent and is a threat to others, the student may need to be removed.

A challenge for the teacher of a power-seeker is to channel the student's need for attention or control in a positive direction. One strategy is to ask the student to collaborate with you. Acknowledge that the student has the ability to lead others and ask for his or her help. Another strategy is to tell the student that his or her disruptions are a problem for you and ask the student to help you solve the problem.

Glaser notes that effective teachers lead rather than boss.[1] He suggests that if students are convinced that what is going on in a classroom is good for them, they will put forth the effort to do quality work. He suggests that the way to convince students of this is to talk to them in a variety of ways, always emphasizing that it is their school. In an earlier work Glaser strongly suggests that coercion is not the way to manage a classroom as it does not provide the proper motivation for students to do quality work.[2]

Counseling is also very helpful in solving the problems of the defiant student. Through counseling the student may come to understand and resolve the issues that have caused his or her need for power and dominance. Many students engage in hostile, defiant behavior with school authorities because they feel inadequate or think that their teachers do not like them. Counseling can help to resolve these feelings.

Additional Reading

Biever, J.L. et al. (1992). Stories and solutions in psychotherapy with adolescents. *ERIC Document Reproduction Service* ED359455.

Charles, C.M. (1992). *Building Classroom Discipline*. White Plains, NY: Longman.

Charney, R.S. (1993). *Teaching Children to Care: Management in the Responsive Classroom*. Greenfield, MA: Northeast Foundation for Children.

Duhon-Sells, R. (1995). *Dealing with Youth and Violence: What Schools and Communities Need to Know*. Bloomington, IN: National Education Service.

Glaser, W. (1992). *The Quality School: Managing Students Without Coercion*. New York: Harper-Collins.

Glaser, W. (1993). *The Quality School Teacher*. New York: Harper-Collins.

Jordan, E. et al. (1995). Knowing the rules: Discursive strategies in young children's power struggles. *Early Childhood Research Quarterly, 10(3)*, 339–358.

McEwan, B., and Nimmo, G. (1995). Effective management practices for severely emotionally disturbed youth: A collaborative study on democratic practices in inclusive classrooms. Paper presented at the annual conference of the American Educational Research Association, San Francisco, CA. *ERIC Document Reproduction Service* ED385045.

---

1. Glaser, W. (1993). *The Quality School Teacher*. New York: Harper-Collins.
2. Glaser, W. (1992). *The Quality School: Managing Students Without Coercion*. New York: Harper-Collins.

Newcomer, P.L. (1993). *Understanding and Teaching Emotionally Disturbed Children and Adolescents*. Austin, TX: Pro-Ed.

Ross, S. et al. (1995). Coping with the student you fear. *Learning*, *24(3)*, 16–17, 22–23.

Case Studies

Case Study #2-1

Student: Bobby

Background: Bobby is a 15 year old eighth grader attending a middle school in a small suburban middle class community. From grade three until grade seven Bobby was placed in a class for emotionally disturbed students. Midway through grade seven he was transferred to a mainstream setting with resource room support and guidance counseling. This change in placement was made at the insistence of Bobby's parents and was contrary to the recommendations of his special education teacher and the school psychologist.

Bobby managed to get through an eight week trial period without any incidents of misbehavior. Academically, he did well in all subjects but his teachers reported that he was disorganized. The resource room teacher assisted him with organization and worked on developing better study skills. Approximately one week prior to the end of the school year he got into a fight with another student who had recently been mainstreamed. Each student was given a three day suspension.

Bobby's eighth grade year got off to a rocky start. His attitude was much more belligerent than it had been the year before. Almost as soon as the school year had started, Bobby got into verbal confrontations with his math and English teachers over his refusal to complete assignments. As the year progressed Bobby's behavior in these two classes worsened. These teachers reported that Bobby totally disregarded any of their directives and, in the words of his English teacher, "did as he damn well pleased." Bobby was sent to the office on an almost daily basis by either one or the other of these two teachers. While at the office Bobby spoke to the principal disrespectfully and conveyed the attitude that nobody was going to tell him what to do. Bobby's other teachers reported that his behavior was not good but had not found it necessary to refer him to the principal for discipline. Although they reported that he was often argumentative, they refused to engage in confrontations with him. Bobby also was failing most of his courses, largely due to his failure to complete assignments. During this time period Bobby was given two suspensions: two days for swearing at the English teacher and three days for fighting. At the suspension hearings Bobby's parents couldn't understand why the school couldn't control Bobby because they were not having any problems with him at home.

Presenting problem: Around Thanksgiving Bobby's behavior reached a critical stage. He started walking out of classes and out of the school building whenever things did not go his way. Whenever he left the building his parents were notified. The principal requested that his parents come to school to discuss Bobby's behavior; however, they refused stating that Bobby's behavior at school was the school's problem. Late in November Bobby was suspended for five days for physically assaulting the English teacher during an argument with him. School officials were particularly concerned about this because the English teacher had a physical disability as a result of war injuries and his ability to defend himself was limited.

While Bobby was out on suspension the school's special education team met with his parents to discuss his Individualized Education Program (IEP) and placement. Bobby's parents were accompanied by a legal advocate. At this meeting they complained that the school had not informed them of Bobby's behavioral problems and if it had they would have been able to do something about it. When presented with copies of letters that had been mailed to them and a log of telephone calls that had been made to them, they denied any knowledge of having received these communications. They also denied having refused to come to school earlier in the month to discuss Bobby's behavior.

Two days later school officials presented Bobby's parents with an IEP calling for placement in an alternative school. The parents indicated that they objected to this placement because they didn't want Bobby to be influenced by the kinds of kids who attended alternative schools. On the advice of their legal advocate they postponed making a decision on the IEP proposal pending the completion of an independent evaluation. For the independent evaluation they chose a facility that was booked three months in advance. The school district allowed Bobby to remain in the mainstream setting but warned his parents that any act of misconduct would result in further suspensions.

Two weeks after returning to school Bobby again assaulted his English teacher. At the suspension hearing, Bobby's legal advocate reminded school officials that he had already been suspended a cumulative total of 10 days that school year, the maximum allowed by state law for a special education student. The special education administrator then sought an injunction from the federal district court to prevent Bobby from attending school until the matter of his IEP was finally settled. The court, finding Bobby to be a danger to others, granted the injunction. The judge gave Bobby's parents two choices: he could attend the alternative school in the interim or he could receive home tutoring.

Questions for reflection and discussion:

1. When Bobby returned to school after the summer recess, school officials noted a change in his attitude from the previous year. What steps should have been taken at that time to prevent the problem from escalating?
2. Bobby's math and English teachers responded to his misconduct by confronting him and having him removed from the classroom. When he committed egregious acts he was suspended. Eventually, Bobby started to remove himself from situations that did not agree with him. All of these actions are ex post facto. What preventative behavioral interventions could have been implemented?
3. Bobby's parents certainly were not overly cooperative in this matter. What steps could have been taken to gain greater cooperation?
4. What role did the legal advocate play? From Bobby's standpoint, was her involvement positive or negative?
5. Was the injunction to remove Bobby from school necessary? Are the two options presented by the judge to his parents reasonable?

Case Study #2-2

Student: Steven

Background: Steven is a 17 year old sophomore who, until recently, attended a vocational-technical high school program for students with special needs. Most of the students in this program have behavioral problems. He is currently living with his mother, his brother's girlfriend, and his one year old nephew. His brother is currently serving time for assault and battery but will be released soon. Steve's parents were divorced when he was six years old because of his father's heavy drinking and abusive behavior. Steve's father served time in another state for armed robbery and credit card fraud but has returned to this area now that he has been released. He is working in the construction field and has promised to get jobs for both Steve and his brother. Steve's mother is not happy about his father's return to the area and, although he appears to be rehabilitated, lives in fear of him.

Steve has been in special education programs since grade three, mostly because of a reading problem. In the elementary school grades he was not considered to be a major league discipline problem even though he managed to get into his fair share of trouble. Steve was somewhat of a class clown and often had to be disciplined for disrupting the class with his antics. However, he was well-liked by his teachers who felt he had a great sense of humor and always tried his best. Even when he became disruptive, he generally could be persuaded to cooperate.

When Steve entered the middle school he developed a reputation for being a discipline problem and eventually was placed in a class for the emotionally disturbed. He seemed to get more frustrated with his inability to read and, as a result, began to act out his anger. Steve started to get into fights, was caught stealing from another student's locker, and was frequently disruptive in class. He frequently refused to complete assignments and, when questioned about these assignments, he became very confrontational. During his middle school years Steve seemed to spend more time in the principal's office than in the classroom. During a suspension hearing that had been called because Steve had destroyed a workbook and smashed his teacher's coffee mug, Steve became enraged when the principal stated that he had a quick temper "just like your brother." Steve responded by punching the principal and had to be physically restrained by his mother, the hearing officer, and the principal. After that incident he was placed on home tutoring for the remainder of the eighth grade.

During the summer Steve was diagnosed at a hospital clinic as having a conduct disorder. The evaluation indicated that he had difficulty with authority figures. The following September Steve entered a vocational special education program and started seeing a therapist at a mental health clinic. Shortly after the school year began his brother's girlfriend and new baby moved into his household. The girlfriend had been disowned by her own family and Steve's mother felt responsible for her since her older son was the baby's father. Unfortunately, a few months before the baby was born Steve's brother started to serve his sentence. In spite of the changes in the household, Steve seemed to adjust well to the vocational school and did not get into any serious trouble that year.

Presenting problem: In early December of his sophomore year Steve engaged in a heated argument with his woodworking teacher who had criticized the project Steve was working on. When he was asked to leave the shop area Steve refused and had to be escorted out. As he was leaving he yelled to the teacher, "You've messed with the wrong guy." He was given a two day suspension but later that day he returned to the school where he was arrested for being in possession of a loaded revolver on school property. He insisted that he had no intention of using the revolver but could not give any reasons for carrying it. He was expelled for the remainder of the year and was given two hours of home tutoring a day. Criminal charges were also filed and Steve was placed on probation. The court also ordered him to continue counseling. Steve has expressed a desire to return to school saying that he realizes that he needs an education. He has also admitted that he "screwed up real bad this time." He does not like the tutoring although he gets along well with his tutor. Steve will be allowed to return to school in September, but the school district has proposed a transfer to an alternative school. Steve does not want to go to the alternative school but rather, wishes to return to the vocational school program. Steve's lawyer has proposed that he be allowed to return to the vocational school with the understanding that he will be transferred to the alternative school if he commits a singe suspendable offense. Steve and his mother are willing to sign an agreement to that effect. School officials have balked at that proposal claiming that Steve has clearly demonstrated that he is dangerous.

Questions for reflection and discussion:

1. What is the source of Steve's anger? To what extent does his reading problem, and consequent frustration, play into his angry feelings?
2. To what extent does the family's history of violence and deviant behavior contribute to Steve's own behavior?
3. What factors led to Steve's outburst in the wood shop? He stated that he had no intention of using the gun. Given Steve's history, can he be believed?
4. Steve appears to realize that his actions were inappropriate and that he needs to straighten out or he may end up in the same situation as his father and brother. Should he be given the opportunity to prove himself by returning to the vocational school program? Is the agreement Steve and his mother proposed reasonable?
5. If Steve returns to the vocational school should any other contingencies be placed on his re-enrollment? What services should he be provided with to help him meet the terms of the agreement?
6. If Steve is enrolled in the alternative school, what should he be required to do in order to earn his way back to the vocational school?

Case Study #2-3

Student: Chris

Background: Chris is a four year old student attending an integrated pre-school class in the public schools. Prior to attending this class she had attended a sectarian day care center and nursery school program. Chris lives with her 22 year old mother and 36 year old step-father in a very affluent neighborhood. Chris' step-father owns his own business and her mother is not employed but does do the bookkeeping for her husband's business. Her father is also remarried and she spends every other weekend and two weeks in the summer with her father and step-mother. She also spends two weeks every summer visiting her paternal grandparents. Academically Chris appears to be very capable. She has been exposed to a wealth of enrichment experiences and is already beginning to recognize a few sight words. She was referred to the pre-school program because of behavioral issues that include stubbornness, poor peer relations, and temper tantrums when she doesn't get her own way. Chris has an Individualized Education Program to address behavioral and social issues.

Problems surfaced almost immediately after Chris enrolled in the preschool program. She was unable to share with other students or play cooperatively with them. She would not take direction from either the teacher or aide. For example, if asked to go to a particular learning center, she would refuse stating she wanted to go to a different center. When disciplined she would pout, stamp her feet, and refuse to cooperate. A conference with her parents was held but her parents seemed at a loss regarding her behavior stating that they had not experienced similar behavior at home. It was learned, however, that Chris did not have any neighborhood friends and spent most of her time either alone or with adults.

The situation escalated when Chris began to get physically aggressive with other students. She would take things away from them and would hit them if they protested. When the teacher tried to explain that she had to share, Chris simply said that the other kids were mean to her. On one occasion Chris stated that she could take anything she wanted because the other kids were scum. When Chris was put in the time out area for taking things away from other students she responded by saying, "I don't care, my grammy will buy me anything I want."

Chris also started to become aggressive with adults in the pre-school. One day she hit the teacher as the teacher tried to direct her to the time out area. On another occasion she hit the aide with a plastic building block because the aide told her to give it back to the student she had taken it from. The guidance counselor contacted the nursery school Chris had previously attended to see if they had experienced similar behavior. The director of the nursery school indicated that it had been an ongoing problem. Their method of dealing with the problem was to redirect Chris to another activity or provide her with one to one attention from an aide. It seemed that they were able to control her outbursts by giving her the attention she demanded.

Presenting problem: Another conference was held with Chris' mother. Mrs. L. was informed that the preschool staff considered Chris to be a danger to other students and that she would need to be removed if her behavior did not improve. A plan was developed whereby Mrs. L. would be called to come pick Chris up anytime she became violent. This plan did not work out, however. Mrs. L. picked Chris up on two occasions, but after that insisted that she did not have transportation when contacted. On one occasion when she was unable to come to the school she asked if she could speak to Chris. Chris refused to come to the phone. At the conference the school psychologist suggested family therapy. Chris' mother initially balked at that suggestion but later indicated that she would look into it. The family did go for an in-take interview but never followed through with the counseling, claiming that their insurance would not cover it.

The final straw came one day when Chris grabbed another student by the neck and shook him. The teacher had to physically remove Chris' hands from the other student's neck. Chris responded by kicking the teacher to the point that the teacher had to put her in a four point restraint. After 30 minutes when it appeared that Chris had calmed down, the teacher released her. At this point Chris turned around and spit in the teacher's face. When Chris' mother was called to take her home, she insisted that her car was in the garage. When it was suggested that she call a cab she said she didn't have the money for cab fare. The preschool director offered to pay for the cab. When Mrs. L arrived at the school Chris greeted her by saying, "I want you to call the police and have these people arrested."

Questions for Reflection and Discussion:

1. Chris appears to be a very determined child who is accustomed to getting her own way. How can the staff at the preschool effectively deal with this?
2. At one point the school psychologist suggested that the family investigate family therapy. Unfortunately this never materialized. How could family therapy have helped? Would it have been helpful to enroll Chris in a play therapy group?
3. What behavior modification techniques could have been employed in the preschool classroom to address Chris' behavior? What is the likelihood of success?
4. A plan had been implemented to have Chris' mother remove her from the preschool whenever she became violent. Was this a wise plan? When the plan failed due to Chris' mother's refusal to come pick her up, how should the staff have responded?
5. To what extent, if any, has Chris' mother abdicated her role as a parent?

Case Study #2-4

Student: Pam

Background: Pam is a six year old first grader attending an inner city elementary school. She lives at home with her mother, her older brother, her twin sister Paula, and her mother's boyfriend. An older sister lives with an aunt. Pam's father has remarried and visits every weekend. Pam's mother was recently found guilty of statutory rape for having had an affair with a teenage boy. She is currently free pending an appeal of her conviction. The Department of Social Services will not become involved because there is no evidence that the mother has abused or neglected her own children. The girls' father, however, is currently trying to gain legal custody.

Pam and her sister Paula attended a special education preschool program and were enrolled in a self-contained special education class for kindergarten. The special education class was not located in their neighborhood school. When they entered the special education class they had not established individual identities to the point that they did not even know which one belonged to which name. In the second half of the kindergarten year they were mainstreamed; however, at the end of the school year the kindergarten teachers felt that the mainstreaming had not been successful. In spite of the kindergarten teachers' misgivings about the prognosis of success in a regular classroom, the girls were returned to their home school to attend a regular first grade with resource room support, as this was the recommendation of the majority of the evaluation team and their mother concurred.

The girls' Individualized Education Programs (IEPs) for the first grade called for them to receive two hours per day of resource room services in reading and language arts, one hour per week of speech and language therapy, and one counseling session per week. They were placed in separate first grade classrooms. Although their math skills were on grade level, individual achievement test scores placed them between the first and fourth percentiles in reading and spelling. Their oral language skills were approximately on a three year old level. They did not use word endings, often omitted words in sentences, and used inappropriate syntax. For example, if one of them needed to use the girls' restroom, she might say to the teacher, "Me go bathroom?" Pam's overall academic skills were slightly higher than Paula's.

The twins were blessed with a good sense of humor. They were quick witted and frequently offered a humorous comment to the classroom routine. They were particularly funny when they were together. The problem, however, was that they did not know when to turn the humor off. They seemed more interested in being funny than in learning. They also did not know what was appropriate classroom humor as opposed to street humor. For example, one day when the class was getting too noisy, Pam's teacher tried to quiet them down by saying, "Excuse me, class." Pam responded, "What, you fart?" The teacher was not amused.

Both girls were very active and did not seem to understand classroom rules and regulations. When disciplined they acted as if they did not understand why their behavior was inappropriate. In general, they seemed very unaccustomed to having limits placed on their behavior. Paula had an easier time adjusting to the first grade than Pam. In part this may be due to basic differences in their personality styles. Paula was more compliant and not as bold as Pam. Pam was the more dominant twin.

Presenting problem: Pam's teacher left on maternity leave mid-way through the year and was replaced by a substitute who had just finished student teaching in December. Pam had difficulty making the adjustment and the teacher, inexperienced in behavior intervention techniques, had difficulty adjusting to Pam. As Pam's oral language skills developed her classroom comments increased. Unfortunately, the inappropriateness of her comments also increased. At first the substitute teacher was shocked by her comments and responded accordingly. This seemed to encourage Pam to make even more outrageous comments. Later, the teacher began to wonder whether or not Pam even realized that her comments and choice of vocabulary were not appropriate for the classroom.

One day Pam asked to go to the bathroom approximately ten minutes after the entire class had been to the bathroom. The teacher told her that she could not go because she had just been there. For the next 15 minutes or so Pam was quite fidgety. When the teacher asked her what the problem was, she informed her, "I have to take a dump." Exasperated, the teacher took Pam to the vice principal and explained the situation. The vice principal looked at Pam and asked, "You wouldn't say something like that at home would you?" Pam wasn't sure. "What would you say if you had to go to the bathroom at home?" the vice principal inquired. Pam thought for a few seconds and replied with a smile, "I have to take a crap." The vice principal was not amused.

A meeting of all staff involved with Pam was called to discuss her behavior and develop a plan of action. It was generally felt that Pam and her sister had been prematurely returned to regular education; however, it was also felt that sending them back to a special education class was not in their best interests.

Questions for reflection and discussion:

1. Does Pam's inappropriate behavior result from an inappropriate educational placement or other environmental factors or both?

2. Is the team's assessment correct that returning Pam to a special education class at this time would be counter-productive?

3. How did the substitute teacher's response to Pam's inappropriate comments escalate the problem? How should she have responded.

4. Most of the staff involved with Pam feel that she is not a bad kid but that she is just undisciplined. What techniques could be used to teach her proper behavior?

5. The staff met to develop a plan of action. What would be the best plan for meeting all of Pam's academic, social, and behavioral needs?
6. Pam is only a first grader. What is likely to happen if her misbehavior is not curbed soon?

Case Study #2-5

Student: Eric

Background: Eric is currently an 11 year old sixth grader attending a middle school with a reputation for being one of the best schools in the state. Eric is the sixth of seven children. His mother had never married and as far as is known her children have four different fathers. The family has been somewhat transient so that Eric has not attended any school system for more than two years. The family is currently contemplating a move to Canada.

Eric's school records indicate that during his elementary school years he experienced some behavior problems but nothing more serious than lying. He received academic support services in reading from a Title I teacher beginning in fourth grade. He is considered to have average intelligence and is not learning disabled. Eric is extremely artistic and prefers to draw most of the time. He carries a drawing pad with him at all times and is often caught drawing in class instead of working on assignments.

Eric's report cards indicate that he is an average student with the exception of his reading problem. Much of his reading problem is attributed to his frequent moves and resultant switching of reading programs. He has not been taught by a consistent method and has developed gaps in his skills. He repeated grade one, due in part to frequent absences. Throughout the rest of his elementary years his attendance was better, but not great.

Eric is now in a departmentalized situation and has four different teachers, two males and two females. He continues to receive Title I support in reading and also receives counseling once a week. His mother has rejected the idea of taking him to counseling at a local mental health clinic with the statement, "There ain't no nuts in my family." Eric started sixth grade off on a positive note but his behavior and academic performance have gradually declined. He has been absent frequently and tardy almost every day he did attend. He shows little respect for his female teachers and has referred to them with inappropriate terminology. He is not cooperative with his male teachers, but does not show disrespect for them. Eric appears to have little interest in his own academic development and tells his counselor that he's going to drop out of school as soon as he's 16 years old. He says he'll make a living picking berries in Canada.

Presenting problem: Recently in class Eric has been assuming the role of class clown. He is willing to do anything to get a laugh from his classmates and shows little fear of consequences. He was recently suspended for three days for an incident in his math class. On one particular day he seemed to have a problem with gas. However, Eric made a big deal out of his problem by dramatically elevating his posterior end into the air and loudly eliminating his gas. This, of course, instigated quite a reaction from the class which only encouraged him to continue. Initially, the teacher ignored his antics; but when they became intolerable she asked him to step outside the classroom. In the corridor she politely explained that she couldn't teach the class with him acting that way and asked him to stop. Eric acted as if he didn't know what she was talking about. Finally, she told him that if he didn't stop disturbing the class in that manner he would have to leave the classroom. At that point Eric responded, "What's the matter Mrs. K., don't you ever fart?" Eric entered the classroom and announced to the class that Mrs. K. apparently never had gas. A few minutes later Eric loudly announced, "I feel a big one coming" and with accompanying dramatics and sound effects continued his award winning performance. Mrs. K. asked Eric to leave the classroom and when he refused, called for the vice principal to remove him. As Eric was escorted from the classroom by the vice principal he insinuated that Mrs. K. supplemented her income in the evening hours. Out in the hallway he yelled as loud as he could, "Hey everyone, don't fart in Mrs. K.'s class or you'll get sent to the office." At the suspension hearing, Eric's only explanation for his behavior was that Mrs. K.'s class was boring. Eric's mother did not feel that he should be suspended and during the suspension period Eric rode his bicycle around the school and laughed at his classmates inside.

A special education class for children with behavior disorders is available within the district. It is located at another middle school and is taught by a female with a female aide. The school district is contemplating evaluating Eric with an eye toward placing him in this class if his behavior does not improve. However, concerns have been raised over whether he would get up in time to get the mini-van in the morning and whether it would be advisable for him to be in a class all day long staffed by two females. Eric has also told his friends that he is planning something to get himself expelled. He says his mother doesn't care if he gets expelled and won't do anything about it. When presented with this information, Eric's mother laughed it off, saying, "What can an 11 year old do to get expelled?" School officials, however, are taking the threat seriously.

Questions for reflection and discussion:

1. Could the incident leading to Eric's suspension have been handled differently? What else could the teacher have done to discourage his antics?

2. Obviously, the suspension was not effective and may even have been counter-productive. What would have been a more appropriate disciplinary sanction?

3. Eric receives counseling in school once a week. At this point Eric is obviously in need of more intensive counseling to find the root of his disrespect for women; however, his mother has refused to take him for outside counseling. What can the school do to see that Eric receives the counseling he so desperately needs?

4. Giving Eric all male teachers is not possible. If it were possible, would this be advisable? What steps can be taken to minimize his disruption in classes taught by female teachers?

5. Does Eric's current behavior warrant the contemplated evaluation and possible special class placement? Would the proposed class be appropriate? What supplemental aids and services could be implemented in his current situation to avoid special class placement?

6. Eric has bragged to his friends that he's going to do something to get expelled. What can school officials do to prevent the commission of an act serious enough to result in an expulsion?

Chapter 3

Revenge and Rage: A Problem Beyond the Traditional Curriculum

In Central Park a short time ago a young jogger was attacked by a roving band of juveniles and savagely raped and beaten with a boulder and left for dead. In Boston, a young teenage mother was attacked by a roving band of more than a dozen juveniles, raped by most of them and stabbed repeatedly dozens of times before being left to die. In St. Louis, a young eighth grader gave birth to a child early in the morning by herself, held the infant until it was time to go to school and threw the child down a laundry chute before heading off to her eighth grade class. In yet another instance a fifteen year old wondered what it would feel like to kill another human being. Shortly thereafter, the teenager lured a classmate into the woods and beat him to death with a baseball bat. A high school senior delivered a baby in the girls' room at her prom, discarded the infant in the trash can, returned to her date after requesting a special song from the orchestra, and proceeded as if nothing unusual occurred.

In writing about the long history of inequity regarding the care of children in the United States, Evelyn Rexford makes the argument that the ambivalence we feel towards children presents a major impediment to our ability to come to terms with what children need from adults.[1] The love vs. hate phenomenon (on the one hand, wanting our children to have everything we did not have growing up, while on the other, feeling that if it was good enough for us then why is it not good enough for them) is a continuous struggle for most adults. Rage and revengeful behaviors by a significant number of young people brings this dichotomy into sharp focus. These behaviors can be seen as the consequence of violent acting out that nightly makes the seven o'clock news.

Unfortunately, these are not isolated instances of aberrant behavior. Researchers and professional care providers who have been studying this behavior for many years have been warning policy makers and other gov-

---

1. Rexford, E. (1976). An American mythology: We care for our children. Keynote Address: Second Child Advocacy Conference of the New England Child Mental Health Task Force. Durham, NH, April 23, 1976.

ernment leaders about these disturbing problems that cut across socioe-conomic levels, reaching in some places epidemic levels. For example, sui-cide incidences among teenagers in various segments of the country, includ-ing individual and group pacts have increased substantially. The significant increase of suicide attempts and fulfillment in the U.S. among teens provides another example of the type of problem driven by rage and revenge. More and more of our young people are choosing a permanent solution to solve a temporary problem. What each of these examples have in common, is that the perpetrators are children and students with experience in classrooms across the United States. They represent a substantially different popula-tion of student needs than at any other time in our history, and yet the models being used to educate the masses have not been changed or improved in the past 150 years.

How do revengeful and rage-like behaviors differ from other behav-iors that are observed and successfully dealt with in classrooms? Just as important, what can be done about them and what do teachers need to know? These are two basic questions that this chapter will attempt to address.

Because words have meaning in reality it is important that one look at the meaning of the terms: *revenge* and *rage*. In the *New Word Dictionary of the American Language*, revenge is defined as to inflict injury or damage, in return for an injury, with great force or fury, excessively to an unusual extent. Rage is defined as a furious, uncontrolled anger, especially a brief spell of raving fury.

From these definitions it is easy to see how difficult, challenging and frightening the presence of any revengeful behavior might be in any class-room. Yet such behaviors are often part and parcel of the developmental frag-mentation that is taking place among groups of students: those who are left at early ages in less than desirable child care arrangements, children who are abandoned through neglect, default, or parental illness and others who are growing up in multi-problem households that have high levels of emotional bankruptcy that result in severe deprivation and lack of support. Howev-er large or small the number is, it is far too many because the great Amer-ican Dream is that every child born in the U.S. is entitled to the most appro-priate public education that will provide each the same degree of opportunity to maximize his/her individual human potential. Yet, policy makers and other governmental decision-makers argue strenuously about the financial and other costs of ensuring that every child be guaranteed his/her right to complete childhood, regardless of how uneven the playing field. Evelyn Rexford's comments regarding the myth of the American belief in the care of children articulates poignantly the pervasiveness of society's ambiva-lence regarding this issue. Collectively we all bear the responsibility and shame for this situation.

For the classroom teachers it is imperative that they do all that they can to avoid experiencing rage and revengeful behavior from their students. The best approach is a preventive one. This can be partly achieved by knowing each student and behaving accordingly. To understand the behavior of others, it is important to understand one's own behavior. In this context the classroom experiences with students are a mirror of the teacher's current behavior. If for example, the teacher is experiencing joy chances are that others in the classroom are experiencing the same emotion. The same can be said about anger, or for that matter any other feeling. One major challenge faced by the responsible adult is the need to always remain in personal control of feelings. Yet, because of social realities of the day such as those described earlier, this is extremely difficult without a great deal of help and assistance on a human resource basis. One of the roles of clinical supervision of interns in medical residence is to monitor the development of personal self-control to insure objectivity. This role continues as doctors seek various specializations in different fields.

Teachers need to develop skills that will permit them to articulate and distinguish behaviors so that others will clearly understand the importance and need for specialized assistance. What are some signposts that one might begin to suggest to accomplish this task? The most crucial is the need to distinguish between various kinds of behavior, some that are clearly attention seeking that test an individual's connectedness, others driven by the need to test power as a way to test personal empowerment, and other behavior that is intimidating, retaliatory and full of hostility.

To help discern behavior one must examine carefully intrinsic motivation to determine cause and effect relationships. Failure to do so risks under-identifying the seriousness of observable behavior in a variety of locations and circumstances. When evidence begins to show the presence of hostility in classroom exchanges this is a time for teachers to become especially sensitive to dynamics and motivation. Hostility is not the same as anger. The latter is a natural emotional response to certain stimuli that disappears as self empowerment is resumed. Not so with hostility that is characterized by clear observable rejection of others, especially adults in charge, such as teachers, as potential allies as well as, inability to take any form of comfort from them as well.

The motivation in these, circumstances is always external from the immediate setting. While a classroom need has provided the triggering of vengeful behavior what often follows is goal displacement. Take for instance a situation involving a child who is being molested by a family member and is too afraid to tell anyone. At recess a smaller peer runs faster in a foot race that the bigger student felt he should have won. To make matters worse the smaller student taunts the bigger peer who reacts only to be confronted by an adult. The over-reaction that takes place borders on mayhem and is completely out of character for this student. Even the presence of a familiar adult is insufficient to restore stability and calmness to the circumstances. In this situation hostility has taken the place of legitimate self-anger over the loss to the smaller peer. What is not clearly evident, however, is the rage the bigger student felt over an external event that became manifested in the over-reaction to losing the race.

When a student is unable to take comfort from a teacher it should be assumed that the child has difficulty with at least some adult relationships. This is also true when there is evidence that adults are not generally accepted as allies. There is the need to help the student clarify emotional reactions to various situations while at the same time bringing to bear other resources that can provide assistance to the child, to the class, and to the teacher. When teachers fail to identify behaviors adequately for which no traditional curriculum activities are appropriate, the result is a disproportionate drain of available quality resources from others that often result in a loss of power and prestige for teacher and students. Teachers who recognize their own professional limitations and communicate such to others contribute to the consciousness-raising initiative calling for full service schools. For such to occur it will require greater leadership behavior from teachers who articulate the needs of their students in a manner that others can understand.

Additional Reading

Abrams, L.A. (1995). Strengthening the fabric of child and family policies: Interweaving the threads of research. In D. Baumrind, *Child Maltreatment and Optimal Caregiving in Social Contexts*. New York: Garland.

Achenbach, T.M. (1975). The historical context of treatment for delinquent and maladjusted children: Past, present, and future. *Behavior Disorders, 1(1)*, 3–14.

Achenbach, T.M. et al. (1991). National survey of problems and competencies among four- to sixteen-year-olds. *Monographs of the Society for Research in Child Development, 56 (3)*, Serial No. 225.

Andeson, J., and Werry, J.S. (1994). Emotional and behavioral problems. In I.B. Pless (Ed.), *The Epidemiology of Childhood Disorders*. New York: Oxford University Press.

Beers, C.W. (1908). *A Mind That Found Itself—An Autobiography*. New York: Longmans Green.

Bender, L. (1948), Genesis of hostility in children. *American Journal of Psychiatry, 105*, 241–245.

Bender, R. (1993). What makes a pull-out program work? *Effective Schools Practices, 12(1)*, 16–19.

Biglan, A. (1995). Translating what we know about the context of anti-social behavior into lower prevalence of such behavior. *Journal of Applied Behavior Analysis, 28*, 479–492.

Boney-McCoy, S., and Finkelhor, D. (1995). Psycho social sequelae of violent victimization in a national youth sample. *Journal of Consulting and Clinical Psychology , 63*, 726–736.

Braden, S.R. et al. (1988). Using punishment with exceptional children: A dilemma for educators. *Teaching Exceptional Children, 20(2)*, 79–81.

Clarizio, Harvey F. (1997). Conduct disorder: Developmental considerations. *Psychology in Schools, 34*, 253–265,

Colvin, G., Ainge, D., and Nelson, R. (1997). How to defuse defiance, threats, challenges, confrontations. *Teaching Exceptional Children, 29(6)*, 47–51.

Comer, J.P. (1988). Is "parenting" essential to good teaching? *NEA Today, 6(6)*, 34–40.

Delpit, L. (1995). *Other People's Children: Cultural Conflict in the Classroom.* New York: New Press.

Eisenberg, L. (1984). The epidemiology of suicide in adolescents. *Pediatric Annals, 13*, 47–54,

Howe, K.R., and Miraniontes, O.B. (1992). *The Ethics of Special Education.* New York: Teachers College Press.

Kanner, L. (1962). Emotionally disturbed children. A historical review. *Child Development, 33*, 97–102.

Meadows, N., Mello, K.J., and Yell, M.L. (1996). Behavior management as a curriculum for students with emotional and behavior disorders. *Preventing School Failure, 40(3)*.

Shanker, A. (1995). Classrooms held hostage. *American Educator, Spring*, 8–13, 47–48.

Steinberg, Zina, and Knitzer, J. (1990). How to look and what to ask: Improving the classroom life of children with behavioral and emotional disorders. *Preventing School Failure, 34(3)*, 4–10.

Case Studies

Case Study #3-1

Student: Fred

Background: Fred is the youngest of three brothers. Shortly after his birth, his parents started using drugs and alcohol. This led to a slow decline which eventually culminated in a series of robberies to support their addictions. Eventually, when Fred was two, his father was arrested and incarcerated. He returned to the home when Fred was nine, but returned to prison shortly thereafter on a parole violation. A maternal aunt came to live with the family when Fred was ten, but she died six months later. In that short period of time, however, she assumed a parenting role. His older brothers are not currently living in the home.

Fred, who is currently in the ninth grade, is a fairly bright student and an avid reader. Unfortunately, however, he often used books as a means of avoiding contact with peers and adults. His interests include small animals, fishing, and playing computer games. Other children in the neighborhood shun him because their parents often refer to his mother as a drunk and his father as a jail bird. As a result of the family situation, Fred receives very little supervision at home.

Fred began exhibiting academic and behavioral problems in the fifth grade. He was placed in a self-contained special education program for the full day. He repeated sixth grade, remaining in the self-contained classroom.

Presenting problem: When he entered seventh grade, Fred was mainstreamed in some academic subjects. However, mainstreaming was reduced when he became aggressive in both his special and regular education classes. He frequently refused to do his work, withdrew from interactions with his peers and adults, made distracting sounds in the classroom, defaced school property, and raced through corridors.

During this time the family situation deteriorated. The landlord evicted the family for non-payment of rent. For a time Fred and his mother stayed with friends and then began living in a car. They are now staying at a shelter.

One week ago Fred was suspended for threatening another student with a knife. As a result of this incident he will be transferred to an off-campus alternative school for 45 days. School officials have scheduled a meeting to determine if Fred's misconduct was a manifestation of his disability and to develop a long-term treatment plan.

Questions for reflection and discussion:

1. What factors should the team consider in determining whether Fred's misconduct was a manifestation of his disability? What additional assessments or information are needed?
2. What environmental factors contributed to Fred's behavioral problems? How have these influenced his personality development?
3. Should school officials have anticipated the escalation of Fred's misbehavior? What proactive steps could they have taken to prevent the knife incident from occurring?

4. What components should be included in a long-range treatment plan for Fred?

5. What outside (i.e. social service) resources are needed to augment Fred's educational program?

Case Study #3-2

Student: Anthony

Background: Anthony is a 15 year old physically strong, muscular ninth grade alternative school student who has a history of anti-social and aggressive behavior toward male authority figures. This behavior has involved him in the juvenile court on many occasions. In the eighth grade he had assaulted two male teachers and the Dean of Students during an altercation that led to assault charges being filed by the school on behalf of the teachers. At that time the juvenile judge filed the case because of lack of sufficient evidence. In fact, the judge let the school staff know that he was not pleased that they would take up the court's time in such matters when school administrative remedies had not been exhausted. After all, the alternative school served special needs students, many of whom had histories of behavior problems. According to the judge, teachers know what risks are involved in working with this population.

Regarding this incident, Anthony had claimed that another student had stolen a watch that his father had given him and he was only trying to retrieve it. In his view the incident was not of his making but had gotten out of hand. Anthony's parents were divorced and the watch had much sentimental value to him. The judge decided to give Anthony a break this time, told him so and advised him not to appear before him again. For several months Anthony displayed no adverse behavior, was cooperative in all classes and with staff, and engaged in healthy competition academically with classmates

Throughout his schooling Anthony has been a fairly good student academically. He has attended school regularly, and in general is regarded as a conflict-free learner, even though there are other issues of concern imposing on his social and emotional growth. Teachers give varying descriptions of Anthony. Females usually see him as courteous, polite, eager to help, gentle in manner, most pleasant, and in general describe him as a good, dependable student. Male teachers, on the other hand, describe Anthony as manipulative, overly suspicious, and cunning. They feel that his competitiveness is really a mask for anger, hostility, and rage. In general the male teachers are uncomfortable around Anthony and warn that he is a powder keg ready to explode. They are at a loss, however, to explain the difference in his behavior with female staff.

Presenting problem: Each year the alternative school held a spring festival with many different kinds of events for students to participate in, including: bag races, track and field events, pitch and throw, and one-on-one basketball. Anthony competed well in most events; however, he lost the 50 yard dash, which he had trained hard for, to a much smaller, less capable, and somewhat physically undersized student. Anthony was upset that he did not win and when another student began to tease him playfully, Anthony lost control and attacked the student physically. Several female teachers attempted to intervene along with the physical education teacher, Mr. Johnson, with whom Anthony had a fair relationship. Mr. Johnson was an imposing man, a former All American linebacker during his college days, and was well-liked by students. However, students knew that he was a no-nonsense teacher and was one to reckon with whenever he became angry.

As staff attempted to calm Anthony down he, without warning, struck out at Mr. Johnson, punching him solidly on the right side of his face. The punch caught him flush on the jaw bone and sent him reeling backwards. The sound of bone cracking could be heard across the field some fifty yards away. Several male staff who had been observing the situation at a distance moved forward quickly to render assistance. Anthony was physically subdued by the staff into a four point restraint, and while lying in this position, yelled at Mr. Johnson, "I finally fixed your ass, didn't I?"

Mr. Johnson was brought to the hospital by one of his fellow teachers. After examination he was released, but advised to take it easy for a few days. His jawbone was very tender and sore, but fortunately, was not permanently damaged.

Anthony was suspended from school and assault charges were filed in the juvenile court. Anthony's mother was in the process of moving out of state with her new husband. She was quite upset that Anthony would cause her further problems at this time. She arranged for Anthony to stay with his maternal grandmother until his legal problems were settled. When Anthony was told of these arrangements, he responded with, "She really screwed me over this time, didn't she?"

Questions for discussion and reflection:

1. Given what is now known, should anything else have been done for Anthony earlier? What should happen to Anthony? What is the justification for such action?
2. How does power interact with revenge and range in this scenario?
3. Who is Anthony's rage directed toward? Why?
4. What kinds of supports are needed for Anthony? If Anthony transfers to another school, what information should go with him?
5. Could the incident described above have been prevented? If so, how?

Case Study #3-3

Student: Christina

Background: Christina is 10 year old fourth grader who lives with her mother and 12 year old brother in an older suburban subdivision. Her parents divorced three years ago and her mother has never remarried. Her father, however, recently remarried. Unfortunately, he married the mother of Christina's best friend, Amanda. He now lives around the corner from Christina with his new family.

Since his remarriage, Mr. Walsh has had little contact with Christina and her brother. He spends all of his time with his new family. Since they live close by, Christina often sees him doing things and going places with Amanda and her two siblings. Christina was very crushed a month ago when he forgot her birthday. Mr. Walsh has also missed several alimony and child support payments. This has put a strain on the family's finances and has meant that they have had to do without a few things.

In the past Christina had been an average student, but this year her grades have been slipping. Concerned that the domestic situation may be having an adverse effect on Christina's achievement, the first Mrs. Walsh asked the school adjustment counselor to have a few sessions with Christina. She confided in the counselor that she missed her dad and was very jealous that Amanda had all his attention. She admitted that sometimes she felt very angry and wanted to do something very mean to Amanda.

Presenting problem: Amanda, whose own father abandoned the family several years ago is thrilled to have a new father in her life. Unbeknownst to the staff, Amanda has been telling Christina about all the things she does with her "new dad." She has also been bringing expensive new toys to school and telling Christina that Mr. Walsh bought them for her.

This morning Amanda forgot her sneakers for her physical education class. Mr. Walsh brought them to her. As he left the school he gave Amanda a big hug and told her that he loved her. Unfortunately, Christina witnessed this interaction. In fact, she was sure that Mr. Walsh had seen her, but he never even spoke to her. Christina naturally felt very hurt.

During the physical education class Amanda bragged that her new dad had bought the sneakers, which were a top brand, for her. Christina had reached the boiling point. She grabbed Amanda by the hair, threw her to the floor, and began kicking her. As Christina was restrained by the teacher, she sobbed, "I'm sick of her rubbing it in my face all the time."

Questions for discussion and reflection:

1. What is the source of Christina's rage? Who is she angry at? Has her rage been misdirected?

2. What can the school adjustment counselor do to help Christina understand her domestic situation? Should she try to approach Mr. Walsh to explain how his actions have affected Christina?

3. How can the school adjustment counselor help Amanda to understand why Christina is so angry?

4. What long-term supports would be necessary or beneficial to help Christina through this crisis? Would family counseling help? Who should attend?

5. What steps can Christina's teacher take to make sure that an incident such as this doesn't reoccur?

Case Study #3-4

Student: Kevin

Background: Kevin is an average student, a fairly good athlete, and quite popular with his peers. However, he has always been in the shadow of his cousin Josh. It seems that no matter what Kevin does, Josh can do it a little bit better. Kevin's father and Josh's father have always been competitive and this has extended down to their children. Report cards and athletic accomplishments are always compared at family gatherings. Kevin doesn't like Josh all that much. He finds him to be too much of a braggart. In fact, if they were not related, he would have little to do with Josh.

Although the two boys live in the same city they attended different elementary schools. However, they now attend the same middle school and this has intensified their rivalry. They are currently in the eighth grade. In October they had each run for student council president. Josh won. Both boys were involved in football and basketball programs. Again, Josh ended the seasons with better statistics than Kevin. Although he has tried his best, Kevin has not been able to bring home the same grades as Josh.

Kevin is beginning to feel the pressure. Earlier this spring they took entrance exams for Latin High School. Both fathers attended Latin, and each wanted his son to follow in his footsteps. Josh was accepted into Latin but Kevin was not. Kevin's father made it clear that he was disappointed and upset at Kevin's failure. He has made a few comments indicating that he doesn't know why Kevin can't excel over Josh at something. He has even stated that he doesn't look forward to the next family gathering because he's embarrassed that Kevin didn't make it into Latin. Although Kevin feels badly that he has disappointed his father, he is really quite happy that he will not be going to the same high school as Josh.

Presenting Problem: The middle school held it's annual "Spring Fling" dance last Friday night as part of graduation week. Kevin had asked one of the more popular girls, Carol, to be his date. Carol had originally accepted, but later changed her mind. By this time it was too late to find another date so Kevin reluctantly went stag.

Kevin was incensed when Josh walked into the gymnasium with Carol. He took a deep breath and went to the other side of the gym. He tried to avoid the couple but somehow they seemed to constantly run into each other. Josh mockingly asked him who his date was and laughed when Kevin said he didn't have one. He felt the rage building inside but just walked away.

When others commented about what a nice couple Josh and Carol were, Kevin just smiled and quietly commented, "Yeah, it's too bad she doesn't know that Josh is gay." He repeated the comment a few more times and then stood back and watched as the rumor quickly went around the dance hall. Kevin smiled again. He was quite proud of the ingenious way he had gotten the ultimate revenge.

Questions for discussion and reflection:

1. What factors had led Kevin to resent Josh and feel the need to seek revenge? What attitudes are present in this situation?
2. How have the fathers contributed to each boy's personality development and feelings of adequacy or inadequacy?
3. Is the spreading of a false rumor, for purposes of revenge, an act of personal violence?
4. Although this incident occurred at an extracurricular activity, how can it affect classroom management?
5. If school officials become aware of what Kevin has done, how should they handle the situation?

Case Study #3-5

Student: Ryan

Background: Ryan is fifteen years old and in the tenth grade. Until recently, he had been a motivated student who had earned average to above average grades. He has always had some difficulty making friends, and as far as anyone can recall, he has always been somewhat of a loner. He did have one close friend, Margie who had been his girl friend since the seventh grade. They had been inseparable until her untimely death just a few month ago from a form of cancer. She had not been sick for long as her illness came upon her and advanced quickly. Ryan, other than showing a visible appearance of sadness, has not been known to have cried since Margie's death. He did attend the wake and funeral but remained aloof from both family and friends, and his presence there was noted as being uneventful. Her death has had an adverse effect on many other people in the community, not only because she was so young, but also because she was well thought of by many. Margie had been involved in volunteer and charitable work. Her family members were all very active in the community. Shortly after Margie's death, Ryan started to show several disturbing behaviors. His attendance at school became infrequent and his grades began to show the effects of his absenteeism. When he did attend school he spent a lot of his time seeking out and picking fights with some of the most troublesome students. He would follow such a student, mimicking and shouting taunts. Even when the student's friends were around, Ryan would invite him to fight. Ryan continued this behavior even though he was frequently beaten up. The school security guards were called on numerous occasions, but generally Ryan's classmates were able to bring peace so that when the guards arrived there was little evidence of any wrong doing.

Ryan resisted all attempts by his peers to befriend him, especially Margie's friends who made many efforts to reach out to him. They attempted to help, even though many were not comfortable with Ryan's eagerness to get involved with the more difficult students in the school. In fact, some of them referred to Ryan as having a death wish. He resisted their efforts by ignoring their overtures and withdrawing, or avoiding places where they were likely to be. In fact Ryan began staying home during the day when his mother and father were out of the house. They both worked long hours at a local paper company. At night Ryan had been observed walking with his dog by the local police. They had become concerned that he was always dressed in black. He generally looked disheveled, wore an oversized long black coat, and his hair had grown long. In general he gave the appearance of someone to be concerned about as a person to be preyed upon or someone who might prey upon more vulnerable others. While Ryan had not broken any laws he was the subject of much talk among the local police who were instructed to be watchful of his presence. There was lots of talk among the police officers about why the city school officials didn't try to do something about this boy with all the local resources that they had.

Presenting problem: Ryan was found early one morning sitting in the middle of a busy intersection. It seems that he just decided to walk half-way across the intersection and just sat in the middle of the roadway. A passer-by called the police on a cellular phone. When the police arrived Ryan became belligerent and attacked the police shouting that they would have to shoot him. Even after he was subdued and calmed down, he continued to ask for someone to please shoot him dead. His appeal was so moving and full of sincerity that even the most hardened officers were concerned about Ryan's well being. When notified, Ryan's parents were beside themselves and not sure what they should do. After consulting with a lawyer, they encouraged the police to file charges against Ryan so that the court would become involved. Charges of vagrancy were filed that same day, but nothing was mentioned in the police complaint of Ryan's attack upon the officers. They did report however, his insistence to be shot dead. The court appointed psychiatrist advised the judge that Ryan had experienced a psychotic breakdown and was in need of in-patient psychiatric evaluation and care. Such an order was issued.

Questions for discussion and reflection:

1. While this seems to be more of a problem for the medical community at this time, what issues, if they had been addressed earlier, might have changed the outcome? In retrospect could anything have been done to help Ryan so that his breakdown could have been avoided?
2. Was it in any way significant that Ryan showed no real overt grief at the time of Margie's death? Could anything have been done at that time to help Ryan deal with his feelings?
3. In what ways is grief important to adolescent development? How is adolescent grief appropriately displayed?
4. Were there any signposts that Ryan was developing psychological difficulties that might have needed attention? Who should have observed such behavior? Why do you identify these individuals'? What should they immediately have been expected to do? Why?
5. Should the high school have a grief plan to address such circumstances? Why or why not?
6. What do you think Margie's friends meant by saying that Ryan had a death wish?
7. What should school officials do when Ryan eventually returns to school? What services will he require?

Chapter 4

Poor Self-Esteem: The Consequences of Stress

Thomas Bergeron, the school psychologist, was quite concerned about Dennis, a student he had seen today. Dennis was a ninth grader who had been referred to him because he was failing most of his major subjects and didn't really seem to care. Although Dennis had never been a great scholar, he had never failed before. His teachers reported that lately he seemed to be down all the time.

In his ten years as a school psychologist, Tom had never encountered a student who thought so little of himself as Dennis. In an interview Dennis had attributed many weaknesses to himself but could not identify a single strength. Dennis was also unable to name another student that he considered to be a friend, saying that no one really liked him very much. In describing himself, Dennis used terms such as "clumsy, geek, nerd, dumb, ugly," etc. He had practically come right out and said that he thought he was worthless.

Tom knew that in order to help Dennis, he had to find the cause of his poor self-esteem. He needed to do a few more personality tests, but based on his initial interview and review of Dennis' school records he was perplexed. Dennis seemed to come from a typical middle class family. His parents were divorced but each had remarried. Dennis stated that he liked his step-father and that his step-mother was "O.K." Although he lived with his mother and step-father, he was able to visit his father and step-mother frequently. An important piece to the puzzle was missing and Tom had to find it. Tom also knew he was running out of time. Dennis was already showing signs of clinical depression and Tom needed to intervene before a crisis developed.

Students who suffer from a poor or lowered self-esteem frequently act out in class to hide their feelings of inadequacy. The classic example is the student with poor academic skills who will misbehave in class to mask the fact that he or she cannot keep up with the rest of the class. This student would rather be viewed by his or her peers as "bad" than as "stupid." Students suffering from low self-esteem may also be suffering from anxiety. Anxiety itself is an assault on self-esteem. Furthermore, the pressures of trying to be accepted, and the awareness that one is not accepted, can cause tremendous stress on children and adolescents.

Students with a poor self-esteem suffer from high anxiety to a much greater extent than their peers. Children who do not feel accepted or loved feel very threatened by their environments and people and events within those environments. These students are concerned about how they are viewed by their peers and adults in their environment. The constant struggle of trying to look good or to hide inadequacies creates a great deal of stress in these students. Stress provokes a number of psychological responses such as repression, rationalization, and denial.

Additionally, students with a distorted self-image may engage in hostile, aggressive, and antisocial behaviors. A child who thinks he is worthless or not as good as everyone else will act accordingly. Frequently these students develop attitudes that are counter-productive to success. In other words the students may think, "Why should I even try if I am going to fail anyway?"

Children are not born with a poor self-image. A poor self-image develops over time. It is usually the result of years of failure and/or rejection. A vicious cycle begins. As the student fails he or she feels less worthy. The lowered feelings of self-worth lead to more failure which just leads to a poorer self-image and so on. Since a poor self-image develops over time, it will take time to correct it. There are no quick-fix solutions to a poor self-esteem.

The task for the teacher, of course, is to gradually build the student's self-esteem while dealing with the resultant misconduct. In this regard, success breeds success. The best way to get any student to develop more positive feelings about himself or herself is to get that student to succeed at something. However, the success must be genuine. The teacher must find ways to build success into the student's daily routine. To do this, the teacher should set realistic goals with the student and then devise a curriculum that will lead toward the attainment of those goals. At the beginning it is best to establish only short-term goals that will be realized quickly. Later, after the student has realized a degree of success, long-term goals may be established.

Students with a poor self-esteem will naturally perform better in a secure educational environment. A secure environment will decrease the stress and anxiety the student feels. A secure environment can be created by finding and emphasizing the student's strong points, giving the student recognition and praise where it is due, and creating tasks in which the student will find success.

Additional Reading

Borba, M. (1989). Esteem builders: A K-8 self-esteem curriculum for improving student achievement, behavior, and school climate. *ERIC Document Reproduction Service* ED347443.

Charles, C.M. (1992). *Building Classroom Discipline*. White Plains, NY: Longman.

Collins, T.W., and Hatch, J.A. (1992). Supporting the social-emotional growth of young children. *Dimensions of Early Childhood, 21(1)*, 17–21.

Gaskin-Butler, V.T. and Tucher, C.M. (1995). Self-esteem, academic achievement, and adaptive behavior in African-American children. *Educational Forum, 59(3)*, 234–243.

Gregg, S. (1996). *Preventing Antisocial Behavior in Disabled and At-risk Students.* Charleston, WV: Appalachia Educational Laboratory.

Gromme-Clark, M. (1995). Creating a positive academic environment for students with behavioral disorders using the Foxfire pedagogy. *ERIC Document Reproduction Service* ED385976.

Hall, R. et al. (1994). The effect of cooperative learning, cross age tutoring and self-esteem enhancing strategies on student behavior and reading achievement. *ERIC Document Reproduction Service* ED371322.

Hess, C.L. (1989). Building self-esteem in boys of elementary school age from alcoholic families. *ERIC Document Reproduction Service* ED311339.

Lee, K.E. (1995). Self-esteem of junior high and high school students. *ERIC Document Reproduction Service* ED387772.

Miller, D. (1994). Using literature to build self-esteem in adolescents with learning and behavior problems. *Clearing House, 67(4)*, 207–211.

Morrow, K.B., and Sorell, G.T. (1989). Factors affecting self-esteem, depression, and negative behaviors in sexually abused female adolescents. *Journal of Marriage and the Family, 51(3)*, 677–686.

Reasoner, R.W. (1994). Self-esteem as an antidote to crime and violence. *ERIC Document Reproduction Service* ED373281.

Sisco, S.S. (1992). Using goal setting to enhance self-esteem and create an internal locus of control in the at risk elementary student. *ERIC Document Reproduction Service* ED355017.

Tanksley, M.D. (1994). Building a good self-esteem for certain fifth grade children through cooperative learning, individualized learning techniques, parental involvement, and student counseling. *ERIC Document Reproduction Service* ED375363.

Vande Kamp, M.E. et al. (1989). Is high self-esteem a precondition of "normal" behavior? *ERIC Document Reproduction Service* ED310331.

Valett, R.E. (1991). Enhancing self-esteem through self-management strategies. *ERIC Document Reproduction Service* ED334496.

Wasserman, T.R. (1988). Improving first grade students' affective behavior through implementing a self-esteem program. *ERIC Document Reproduction Service* ED327274.

Case Studies

Case Study #4-1

Student: Brad

Background: Brad is a 14 year old seventh grader. He repeated the second grade because of a severe reading problem. He was diagnosed as dyslexic in the first grade and has been receiving special education services since that time. When his reading showed little improvement after repeating the second grade, consideration was given to placing him in a self-contained classroom for learning disabled students. This was not done, however, because Brad's math skills were average and there were other students who were considered to be a higher priority for such a placement. Brad lives with his parents and 12 year old brother in subsidized housing. His father works as an unskilled laborer and his mother works part time as a home health aide. Brad's younger brother is an excellent student and an excellent athlete.

Presenting problem: Brad has always suffered from a poor self-esteem. He considers himself to be "dumb" because of his reading disability. Perhaps due to years of failure, he is unwilling to try something if he thinks he won't succeed. His self-esteem was further injured by the fact that his younger brother had surpassed him academically and was a better athlete, a fact that he was constantly reminded of by his brother and his father. Brad's problems became worse when he entered the middle school. For the first time he switched classes. His reading disability made it very difficult for him in his science and social studies classes because he couldn't read the textbooks. He even began to experience difficulty in math because he couldn't read the word problems. Unfortunately, his poor organizational skills also interfered with his success. He had difficulty keeping track of his homework assignments and was constantly losing assignments. Brad was evaluated by a neurologist for attention deficit hyperactivity disorder but the diagnosis was negative. Before his sixth grade year was over, Brad had been placed in all special education classes.

Brad entered the seventh grade with a very poor attitude. He complained to his counselor about being placed in all "retard" classes. He said that he wanted to go to the same classes as his friends. He stated emphatically that if he wasn't allowed to go to regular classes he would quit school. The counselor tried to reason with him to no avail. The counselor finally made an agreement with Brad to put him in a regular education math class. If he did well in that class, the counselor told him they would consider putting him into other regular classes.

At first Brad gave the math class his best effort. However, it proved to be too difficult for him. Rather than admit that he couldn't handle it, he started to act out in class. In front of his friends he acted as though he didn't want to do the work. In class he took on the role of class clown. When the teacher called on him to answer a question, Brad responded with silly answers. His poor behavior also began to spill over into his special education classes where he continued the class clown routine. Brad began to act very macho and told his friends that he was going to drop out at age 16. He started skipping classes and eventually began skipping school. One day the vice principal found him hidden underneath a stairway, kissing a female student. As the vice principal was escorting the two students to the office he commented that Brad seemed to be going downhill fast. Brad told him to go @#$& himself. Brad was given a two day suspension.

Questions for reflection and discussion:

1. How has Brad's lack of academic achievement contributed to his low self-esteem? To what extent has this contributed to his recent behavior problems?
2. Would it have made a difference if the school district had placed Brad in the learning disabilities class when he was in elementary school? Why or why not?
3. Was Brad's transfer back to a regular education math class a mistake? Why or why not? What supports could have been implemented to make it a more successful experience?
4. At this point Brad seems to be at risk for dropping out of school. What can be done to prevent this from occurring?
5. At this point in his life, what can be done to bolster Brad's self-esteem.

Case Study #4-2

Student: David

Background: David is an 11 year old fourth grader attending an inner city school. He lives with his mother, his older sister, and his brother in subsidized housing. David's father lives in a nearby city and the children visit him periodically. His father has remarried and has one child from his new marriage. David's older sister is an honor roll student and her mother's pride and joy. David's mother constantly reminds him that his sister is a much better student and asks him why he can't be more like her. His older brother attends an educational collaborative program for emotionally disturbed students.

David has received resource room services since the third grade to improve his reading, language, and spelling skills. His math skills are close to grade level. He also receives guidance counseling services in school and psychotherapy from a local mental health center. David is a very active student who has difficulty with impulse control: He frequently talks out, has trouble waiting his turn in games, and is very fidgety. When angered David strikes out by throwing things or hitting other students. After an incident David is able to realize that his actions were wrong but insists that he "couldn't help it." A neurologist diagnosed David as having an Attention Deficit Hyperactivity Disorder but a psychiatrist diagnosed him as having an oppositional defiant disorder. Both suggested that stimulant medication might help but David's mother is a recovering drug addict and does not want any unnecessary medications in the house.

Presenting problem: Recently (within the last six months) David's angry outbursts have intensified. His teachers feel that he is more impulsive, in part because he does not try to control his impulses anymore. He has verbally lashed out at teachers with such comments as: "I hate you, you're so mean" and "This school sucks, you can't do anything here." When spoken to about his behavior, he responds with comments such as, "What do you expect from a psycho?"

Other students do not want anything to do with David because he lashes out at them physically when things don't go his way. Unfortunately, not many things go his way. In class he frequently gets out of his seat and wanders around. Often he walks to the window and just stares outside. He ignores his teacher's requests to be seated.

However, the major concern is that David has been lighting fires. He has been caught on two occasions but he is under suspicion for setting others. The first time he lit the school's dumpster on fire. The second time he lit his brother's bed on fire with his brother in it. He is on probation from the second incident.

One day during lunch David climbed into the trash barrel and sat in it. When questioned about this behavior by the guidance counselor, David responded that he was "nothing but trash anyway." Later that day in the resource room David climbed onto a counter and threatened to jump out an open window. He did get off the counter when asked to do so but insisted that he was going to kill himself. He claims that no one likes him and that he is not treated fairly by his mother or teachers.

David's mother has contacted the Department of Social Services and has requested their assistance. She claims that she can no longer handle David and that she fears for her safety and that of her other children. She has asked D.S.S. to put David in a foster home or a residential facility. D.S.S. has agreed to a residential placement and has asked the school district to fund the educational component. The school district has refused, claiming that it has an appropriate placement, a self-contained classroom for emotionally disturbed students. The school district further contends that since the residential placement is not necessary for educational reasons, and is being made strictly for social reasons, that D.S.S. should be responsible for all costs.

Questions for reflection and discussion:

1. David's mother's words and actions suggest that she favors his sister. In any event David certainly feels that his sister is the favorite one and can do no wrong. To what extent, if any, does this contribute to David's lowered self-esteem?

2. Stimulant medication was recommended but rejected by David's mother due to her own involvement with drugs. Is her stance justified? To what extent should school personnel have tried to change her thinking?

3. What types of behavior intervention strategies could have been implemented in the classroom when David's impulsivity increased and his teachers felt that he was no longer trying to control his impulses?

4. Up until now David has been in a regular education program with support services. The school district did not contemplate a special class placement until a residential placement was requested. Could the escalation of David's behavior problems have been averted if a special class placement had been made earlier?

5. Is the school district justified in refusing to cost-share the residential placement?

Case Study #4-3

Student: Scotty

Background: Scotty is a five year old kindergarten student. He is the youngest of three children of a single mother. His older sister attends the school district's middle school program for gifted and talented students. His older brother is a fourth grader at the same school and is an average student. Several of Scotty's cousin's attend the same school. One of his cousins, Emily, is in a special education class for developmentally disabled students.

Scotty is a very quiet child but is prone to violent temper tantrums. On many occasions, apparently without provocation, he has started to throw things around the classroom. One time he pulled everything off a bookshelf and had to be physically restrained. After each of these incidents, Scotty has been unable to verbalize why he acted in this manner. When his behavior has been particularly uncontrollable, he has been sent home for the remainder of the day. Scotty's mother has told him that if he doesn't "smarten up" he'll end up in Emily's class.

On an almost daily basis Scotty destroys a worksheet or a coloring paper by scribbling all over it. When this occurs his teacher has tried to redirect him without success. Again, he is unable to explain why he is so angry. Scotty also spends much of his day crawling around on the floor. For the most part, however, he does this without disturbing the class.

When he does participate in the class, he appears to be academically appropriate for kindergarten.

Presenting problem: On a recent occasion Scotty drew a picture of what appeared to be an anatomically correct man. After drawing it he scribbled over it and then violently stabbed at the penis area with his pencil.

Scotty was referred to a neurologist who was unable to find a biological cause for his behavior. She referred him to a psychiatrist. However, the psychiatric evaluation was delayed for several months because the psychiatrist had surgery and then Scotty's mother missed two appointments. The psychiatrist eventually diagnosed Scotty as having an adjustment disorder with atypical features. The psychiatrist indicated that there was a strong possibility that Scotty had been sexually abused and that he suffered from feelings of guilt and a lowered sense of his own worth. Intensive psychotherapy was recommended.

The school district is considering a special class placement but the psychiatrist has advised against it. He feels that a special class placement would further make Scotty feel that he is "defective." The psychiatrist has recommended that Scotty remain in a regular class situation but that a counselor be available to provide crises intervention when needed. The psychiatrist has also advised the school that Scotty shouldn't be sent home when he misbehaves because that only reinforces his poor self-esteem by giving him the message that he is not worth dealing with.

Questions for reflection and discussion:

1. What could be the source of Scotty's anger? Why is he unable to verbalize his reasons for his actions?
2. Is the psychiatrist correct that a special class placement could further damage Scotty's self-esteem?
3. If Scotty is placed in a regular first grade classroom next year, what supplementary aids and services should he be provided with in addition to the crisis intervention counseling?
4. What behavioral techniques could be implemented by Scotty's teacher in the regular classroom to control his behavior?
5. Is the psychiatrist correct that sending Scotty home when he misbehaves contributes to the problem by sending him the wrong message?

Case Study #4-4

Student: Brianna

Background: Brianna is an 11 year old fifth grader who transferred to the Pine Creek School this past September when her family purchased a home in the area. The Pine Creek School is located in a typical middle class neighborhood and has a reputation for excellence, having won a number of national and state awards. Brianna's father drives a truck for a rubbish disposal company and her mother works as a cashier at a local convenience store. Brianna has an older step-sister from her father's previous marriage and two older brothers. She also has a younger sister. The step-sister has recently moved in with the family after having lived with her mother. Since she is having psychological problems this has created a good deal of family stress.

Brianna was diagnosed as having learning disabilities in the first grade. She has received specialized tutoring in a resource room setting since that time. Although her reading skills have always been significantly below grade level, she has never been retained. Her last Individualized Education Program (IEP) called for her to receive three half-hour individualized tutoring sessions per week.

When Brianna began at the Pine Creek School, the staff was quite concerned about her low reading ability. Her skills were far below other students who attended the resource room program. The special education staff was of the opinion that the services called for in her IEP were grossly inadequate. A decision was made to conduct a thorough re-evaluation.

The staff was also beginning to realize that Brianna had some emotional problems as well. On several occasions Brianna left the school building and ran home when she became upset. For example, one day when the class was working on an exercise to teach them to fill out forms, Brianna tore her practice form up because she could not read it. Her teacher gave her a new form and gave her two options: he would help her complete it or she could bring it to the resource room and complete it there. Brianna threw the second form on the floor and ran out of the classroom crying. She then walked right out the front door and headed for home.

The re-evaluation revealed that Brianna had average intelligence but severe learning disabilities. Her reading test scores were on a second grade level and her spelling scores were even lower. Brianna's math scores were on a fourth grade level. Her inability to do word problems lowered her score in this area.

Psychological testing revealed that she had a very poor self-esteem. She felt very inadequate as a result of her poor reading skills and felt that she was ugly. Furthermore, her self-esteem appeared to suffer a blow when her step-sister moved into the home. Brianna did not fully understand the reasons why her step-sister came to live with the family and felt threatened by all of the attention the step-sister was receiving. Brianna seemed to be unsure of her place in the family. During the testing it was discovered that other students had been teasing her because her father was a garbage man. The psychologist felt that between her home and school situations, Brianna was under a great deal of stress.

When the evaluation and placement team met with Brianna's parents it was decided to place Brianna in a learning disabilities class for all of her reading and language arts instruction. Since the school operated on an inclusion model, Brianna remained in the fifth grade class for home room, math, science, social studies, and health. She also stayed with the regular class for all specialists, lunch, and recess. In all, she spent approximately 40% of her day in the learning disabilities class. The learning disabilities teacher consulted with the fifth grade teacher once a week to develop strategies for meeting Brianna's needs in the classroom. Also, the paraprofessional from the learning disabilities class was made available to the fifth grade teacher on an as-needed basis to adapt materials (such as putting textbooks on audio tape). It was also learned that the family would be attending 10 counseling sessions, the maximum allowed under their health insurance policy.

Presenting problem: Placement in the learning disabilities class went well for Brianna. Since the work was individualized, it was not as frustrating for her. The L.D. teacher also discovered that Brianna had a talent in art and incorporated art activities into many lessons. When the class worked on art projects Brianna was used as an "assistant teacher." Although she was still struggling in the regular classroom, Brianna seemed better able to handle her frustration there. With guidance from the assistant principal, Brianna had reached the point where she would ask to go to the office whenever she felt she was going to lose control. Although all agreed that this was far better than running out of the building, Brianna's classroom teacher felt that she sometimes abused this privilege and used it to get out of assignments she did not want to complete.

With things going better for Brianna, what could possibly be the problem? The problem is that the school year is ending and Brianna is scheduled to transfer to a middle school next year. The staff at Pine Creek wishes that they had one more year to work with Brianna to build on what has been accomplished this past year. They are considering retaining her in grade five because they are concerned that another transition at this time will result in regression and that she is not academically capable of being mainstreamed at the middle school. However, they are also concerned that a retention will further damage Brianna's already fragile self-esteem, especially since it would put her in the same grade as her younger sister. Basically, the options they have are to retain her and keep her in her present program or promote her but place her in a completely self-contained learning disabilities class.

Questions for reflection and discussion:

1. Brianna's classroom teacher is concerned that she may be taking advantage of the privilege of going to the assistant principal's office whenever

she feels she is getting upset. The assistant principal, however, feels that this is a minor trade-off for not having her run out of the building. How can the situation be structured so that Brianna can be given voluntary time-out when needed without an abuse of the privilege?

2. Brianna's placement in the learning disabilities program and her teacher's using her as a leader on art projects has bolstered her feelings about herself. Why have these steps been beneficial? What else could have been done to make Brianna feel good about herself?

3. The family will be attending 10 counseling sessions. Is this sufficient? If not, what can the school's staff do to see that family counseling is continued?

4. The staff at Pine Creek has identified two options: retaining Brianna in grade five or promoting her to a self-contained learning disabilities class at the middle school. Is the staff being myopic? With a little creativity, what other options could be developed that might be better for Brianna?

5. If Brianna is retained in grade five, what steps can be taken to deal with the effect this may have on her self-esteem?

6. If Brianna is promoted to the middle school learning disabilities class, what steps can be taken to provide her with some mainstreaming in sixth grade classes?

Case Study #4-5

Student: Patrick

Background: Patrick is a 10 year old fourth grade student. He has an older sister and a younger brother. His mother became pregnant with Patrick's sister while still in high school. The sister's father was a married man for whose family she had been baby sitting. She married Patrick's father but he walked out on the family before the younger brother was born. Mrs. Bean has since returned to school, earned her diploma, and now works as a manager of a health spa.

After becoming pregnant in high school, Mrs. Bean went to live with her godmother. Her godmother was very generous and provided her with built-in child care. However, instead of returning to school or working, Mrs. Bean spent her time socializing. Consequently she never developed parenting skills. During this time period she became pregnant with Patrick. She moved out of her godmother's house when she married Patrick's father. She was not happy with the second pregnancy, even though Patrick's father agreed to marry her. Abortion was out of the question, however, due to her religious beliefs.

Patrick's father never developed a relationship with him and perhaps resented him. Patrick reacted by constantly craving attention whenever an adult was present. For example he often cried until he was picked up and held. After four years Mrs. Bean became pregnant with Patrick's brother. Mr. Bean was not at all happy with this pregnancy and walked out during the first trimester, claiming that the baby was not his. He has not been heard from since and efforts to locate him to secure child support have failed. To complicate matters, Mrs. Bean's godmother has since passed away, leaving her with no family support system. Mrs. Bean has tried to be a good single mother but finds the responsibility of working and caring for three children overwhelming at times.

Patrick had been involved in a number of minor disciplinary actions since entering school. Academically, he was slightly below average but his conduct and effort grades were always poor. Patrick lost his temper easily, especially if other students teased him. His teachers generally felt that he had a short fuse and for the most part handled him carefully.

Presenting problem: Patrick was brought to the principal's office by his teacher who was totally exasperated. In obvious anger she told the principal she had taken all she was going to and wanted him out of her class. The incident that had been the last straw was that Patrick had stabbed a classmate in the cheek with a pencil, barely missing her eye. The thought of what could have happened was frightening.

The injured girl's parents were also outraged and expressed their feelings very vocally. They threatened to storm the next board of education meeting if something were not done to remove Patrick from their daughter's classroom. They also threatened to send their daughter to a private school and sue for tuition reimbursement if her safety could not be guaranteed in the public schools.

When the principal had spoken to Patrick about the incident he had been quite anxious and angry. When she asked him to lower his voice and speak to her in the same tone she was using to speak to him, he replied, "I don't care about you. I hate you! I hate everybody. No one cares about me anyway." Patrick then sat down and sulked for about five minutes. When the principal tried to speak to him again he shouted, "Don't you know that I wasn't wanted when I was born?" He then started to cry. Finally, he sobbed, "She called me a moron."

"Is that why you stabbed her?" the principal asked. "No," Patrick replied quietly. "I stabbed her when she said, 'Even your mother hates you. My mother told me so.'" Patrick then added, "See, she started it."

Mrs. Bean was called and Patrick was sent home for the remainder of the day. However, before he left Mrs. Bean informed him that his "stupid actions" were causing her all sorts of problems at work. She added that she couldn't afford to devote so much time to him. As she left she muttered, "I wish we could find your father so you could go live with him."

The principal sympathized with Patrick's circumstances. Nevertheless, she had to respond to the incident. She was now faced with the difficult task of explaining to his teacher why she had not taken harsher disciplinary action. She also did not look forward to dealing with the injured girl's parents again. She had very mixed feelings. She understood that Patrick was a victim but also recognized that he had to be held accountable for his actions. She had great difficulty distancing herself from the discipline problem. She also knew that she needed to help Patrick's teacher better understand his needs.

Questions for reflection and discussion:

1. What are the major issues that need to be identified regarding Patrick's behavior and his overall human condition?
2. Can Patrick's behavior be classified as attention-seeking or is it simply a reflection of his low self-esteem? How can his behavior be explained?
3. Would counseling be an appropriate option? What kind of counseling should be recommended? Why?
4. What types of professional development activities could help those who teach Patrick better respond to his needs and behaviors?
5. What other interventions could be designed for Patrick? Consider home or family interventions as well as school interventions.

Chapter 5

Communication Misunderstandings: How Do I Know What You Mean by What You Are Saying?

As Mrs. MacDonald was preparing her lesson plans, her thoughts wandered to her new student, Eric. Eric had only been in her class for a week but already he had encountered difficulties with his new fourth grade classmates. Eric seemed to be having trouble communicating with them and several misunderstandings resulted.

Eric had also misunderstood some of the things Mrs. MacDonald had said to him. At first it was a bit humorous but she was beginning to think he might have a problem. On the first day Eric had been in her class Mrs. MacDonald asked him what book he had been reading in his former school. When Eric told her she asked him how he had found it. Eric had replied, "Oh, Mrs. Johnson just gave it to me." Another day, when Mrs. MacDonald was playing classical music during a break, Eric asked her if she liked listening to "Oprah."

Since kickball games on the playground are not refereed, the students settle disputes by having the two players involved "buck up." The other day when there was a dispute as to whether Eric was safe or out, the captain of the other team called "buck." Eric, whose front teeth protrude, took offense and hit him.

Several of the students have nicknames for each other. Wanting to join in and be accepted, Eric gave his own nicknames to a couple of the students. However, his nicknames were not very flattering and the students were not amused. It certainly was not a good way to start off in a new school.

In this chapter the consequences of well intended messages that have been misinterpreted, resulting in loss of control that create disturbances in the classroom will be discussed. Many difficulties could be avoided through the practice of a validation of meaning approach that uses active listening skills. These are skills that can be taught to students so that they may become sensitive and able to validate message sending, receiving and interpretation. Some of the suggested reading at the end of this chapter will include research on the expectancy phenomena and how teachers communicate their expectations to their students. These readings will also enlighten the teacher on the issues of the hidden curriculum that exists in every class-room which receives little if any direct attention as part of regular teacher behavior. Best practice research strongly suggests that teachers communicate their expectations to students in very uneven, and at times grossly unfair, ways that send different messages to different students depending upon how teachers and students are perceiving one another. What is surprising in the research literature is that rather than teachers being consciously biased as some complain, teachers far too often are unaware of the different styles that are being used in their interactions with students. In other words teachers often communicate expectations in a covert manner without any awareness of the process from student to student.

Much of the research on teaching and learning emphasizes the simple but compelling fact that one approach doesn't fit every student in the classroom. Further, every student in the classroom does not learn at the same rate, same pace, or same level. The one size fits all tradition, in spite of burgeoning evidence to the contrary, is alive and well in many classrooms and schools. Because the model of schooling today is the same as it was a hundred years ago, yet serving a very different population of children, it is not difficult to see why there exists strong support for traditional practices in the absence of strong public policy to the contrary. Developers of charter schools often use this argument in building support for their efforts.

Teachers are becoming more and more aware that their classrooms consist of varied types of diverse learners. Few would deny the importance of knowing more about learning styles that identify how best each of their students assimilate learning of new academic and social behaviors. Recognition of such diversity among classroom groups requires that teachers, in order to provide the same degree of opportunity for each learner to experience success in school, use specific and individual information about their students to plan instruction that increases the attainment of such an outcome. One of the first areas that teachers need to be in control of is the flow of information to and from class members, including the teacher as well. Failure to design and establish criteria against which verbal, written and other forms of communication (such as body language, cuing, signs, dress, rituals, etc.) are viewed, can cause major interpretation problems and misunderstandings. This leads to unnecessary disruption and creates loss of control issues among members of the classroom. While celebrating differences through cultural expressive projects, (such as exhibits, food fairs, etc.) is valuable, it in and of itself does little to inculcate and intensify relationships among students to students and students with teacher that allow for the development of positive attitudes and caring concern for group members in their day to day interpersonal exchanges.

The hidden curriculum components of power, crowds, and praise have strong influence on what happens to each student while learning standard curriculum content. Providing students with skills that empower them to validate the messages that are sent so that they can attach the meaning that is intended can go a long way in reducing the amount of confusion that results in negative consequences. The power that exists within each classroom is a strong source of strength that enables individual autonomy and exercise of personal decision making, so that each participant can demonstrate appropriate behaviors that lead to school success.

Crowds are another component of the hidden curriculum that has a strong influence on what form of growth takes place in the classroom. Structured appropriately, groups can be supportive, encouraging, and stimulating. When little attention is given this dimension of the curriculum, student cliques tend to develop and selective discrimination of certain students results in diminished motivation and lack of initiative on the part of excluded students. As an assault on the student's rightful membership in the total class of childhood, the consequences are usually devastating to the child. Irreparable damage to the child's self worth can result.

In addition to how individuals are perceived by one another, other factors that individuals rely on to interpret messages include the wording of a communication, tone, style, expression, and body language cuing and rituals. While still other factors involve issues of trust in a message and issues of respect in a message. The latter two factors relate to the prior experience and reputation that individuals hold of each other.

Teachers can teach active listening skills through modeling and insisting that students use the demonstrated behaviors in their daily interactions. Such active listening skills include emphasis on validation of what is being communicated by someone else by listening to what is being said, and avoiding judgment of what is being said. The components of active listening skill instruction are: acknowledging, paraphrasing, reflecting by focus on speakers feelings, clarifying what is being interpreted, elaborating based on verbal as well as non-verbal cues, and summarizing as a method of pulling together relevant information that can speak for itself.

Active listening skills can help to validate messages, increase comfort between and among classroom members and can go a long way towards building cooperation and positive learning classrooms. Students and teachers can be confident that the interpretation of messages matches intentions of the sender.

Additional Reading

Axelrod, S., and Apsche, J. (Eds). (1983). *The Effects of Punishment on Human Behavior*. New York: Academic Press.

Banks, J.A. (1993). *Introduction to Multicultural Education*. Boston: Allyn & Bacon.

Baumrind, D. (1995). *Child Maltreatment and Optimal Caregiving in Social Contexts*. New York: Garland.

Belcher, T.L. (1995). Behavioral treatment vs. behavioral control: A case study. *Journal of Developmental and Physical Disabilities*, 7, 235–241.

Bettelheim, B. (1970). Listening to children. In P.A. Gallagher and L.L. Edwards (Eds.), *Educating the Emotionally Disturbed: Theory to Practice*. Lawrence: University of Kansas.

Breitborde, M. (1996). Creating community in the classroom: Modeling new basic skills in teacher education. *Journal of Teacher Education, November-December*.

Dyer, K., and Luce, S.C. (1996). Teaching practical communication skills. *Innovations: AAMR Research to Practice Series*, No. 7.

Sugawara, Y., and Peterson, C. (1994). Communicative competence: The cultural factor in language training. *ERIC Document Reproduction Service* ED371414.

Rancer, A.S. (1990). Argumentativeness and verbal aggression: Their role in family violence and cross-cultural communication. *ERIC Document Reproduction Service* ED322539.

Case Studies

Case Study #5-1

Student: Sarah

Background: Sarah is an enthusiastic fifteen year old tenth grader who has recently transferred to East High School. She was enrolled by a social worker, Mrs. Thomas, who claimed to be Sarah's appointed Guardian. Prior to Sarah's enrollment, Mrs. Thomas met briefly with Mr. Fernandes, the guidance counselor assigned to Sarah, to provide Sarah's personal background information for the school's records. Mrs. Thomas informed him that until recently, Sarah had been living in a foster placement with Mr. and Mrs. Burns along with three other foster children including a sixteen year old and two babies, eighteen and nine months old respectively, none of whom are biologically related. Sarah was removed from this placement four months ago and went through a series of placements and treatment centers to receive help for acute behavioral problems, ranging from psychotic episodes to manic depressive disorders. She had been on psychotherapeutic medications over the past six weeks which improved her behavior and stabilized her to the point where doctors felt her suitable for placement in a less restrictive setting. Thus, she was encouraged to attend a local high school in the community. Mrs. Thomas also reported that Sarah has always enjoyed school, was very popular, and always found learning exciting. Her favorite subject being science, Sarah decided she might like to become a nurse and has also entertained the thought of becoming a journalist because of her love for English.

Remarkably, Sarah tested in the near gifted range, scoring a 127 on an IQ test and has, for the most part, been a cooperative student, gotten along well with most teachers who challenged her, has received good grades, and was liked for both her spirit and her enthusiasm. Her behavior inconsistencies never surfaced while in a school setting. Mrs. Thomas also stated that the bulk of this information about previous schooling came from a third party interviewee (a former social worker), over the telephone. Sarah's turbulent prior history and infrequent school attendance resulted in very poor and inaccurate school records that attempted to explain her situation. Indications suggested that Sarah missed considerable amounts of school within the last several years.

Presenting problem: Several weeks after Sarah's matriculation at East High, the school Principal, Ms. Malone, received a troublesome phone call from a staff attorney at the District Attorney's office of Fernwood County. Ms. Malone was told that Sarah was a suspect in the rather bizarre death of a youngster who resided in the same foster home where Sarah had lived, and informed her that he would like to visit the school to interview Sarah. While no formal charges had been filed against her, the school staff was alerted to be wary of anything that Sarah might say to teachers and to other students which could help with the investigation. Also, she decided that school records must be well documented in the event that school officials would be called to court at a future date. Ms. Malone informed the attorney that she must speak with her superintendent for guidance before allowing any visits or interviews on the school premises.

During her meeting with the school superintendent, Ms. Malone was directed to meet with Mr. Fernandes to see if he could shed any light on this situation with Sarah. Mr. Fernandes was surprised, shocked, and somewhat outraged that Sarah's guardian painted such a rosy picture about Sarah's behavior. A meeting was proposed to help clarify the situation and to get to the bottom of what was going on. Mr. Fernandes was to arrange for such meetings to take place off school grounds. In the meantime, the superintendent was convinced that it would be in everyone's best interest if no contact at all were permitted with outside agency people until after he consulted legal counsel for advice.

The following day, the local newspaper carried a story alleging that the fifteen year old girl was suspected of foul play in the death of a foster brother. When the school day began, the phone was ringing off the hook with complaints from some very concerned parents.

Questions for reflection and discussion:

1. What are some of the issues that school officials are dealing with here? How should Sarah be treated by her teachers? How can they deal with the anticipated reaction by her peers?
2. How have Sarah's severe behavior problems impeded her ability to perform and function in school and in society?
3. How has poor communication (i.e. misinformation, lack of information) impeded the school's ability to help Sarah?
4. What else could school officials have done to obtain information about Sarah when she was enrolled so that the current dilemma would have been avoided?
5. What kind of counseling, or other academic and emotional support services, will help Sarah deal with her overall situation?
6. What steps can school officials take to make sure that something like this does not happen again?

Case Study # 5-2

Student: Lauren

Background: Lauren is a senior attending a magnet school for gifted and talented students. She has applied to, and expects to be accepted to, several ivy league colleges. She hopes to major in English Literature with the intent of someday being a writer.

Lauren is literally a success story. Her mother is an alcoholic who has been in and out of many institutions. Her father is a state senator who spends the majority of his time in the state capital. He has ambitions to be the governor. Lauren's mother has been her primary caretaker; however, she has spent a considerable amount of time living with relatives during her mother's bad times. Consequently, she attended six different elementary schools and two middle schools. Fortunately, she has been able to attend the same high school for four years.

As a child Lauren experienced psychological and emotional problems. However, thanks to many years of psychotherapy, she is now fairly stable. She has not received any counseling or therapy in the past four years. In spite of her emotional difficulties and constant school changes, Lauren managed to achieve at an average to above average level throughout her schooling. She was accepted into the magnet school on a provisional basis, based on the recommendation of one of her middle school English teachers. That teacher had recognized that Lauren had a special aptitude for writing. The magnet school seemed to be just the thing Lauren needed, as she has excelled in her four years there. In addition to being academically inclined, Lauren is in the school band and is a fairly good basketball player.

Presenting problem: One of Lauren's classmates informed the English teacher (who was known affectionately to his students as Mr. Chips) that Lauren had stolen a paper that she had written and had passed it in as her own work. Mr. Chips re-examined the paper and determined that its quality was not typical of what he had come to expect from Lauren. He concluded that Lauren had probably not written the paper.

Mr. Chips called Lauren in for a conference. He told her that he had some concerns about her latest paper because it was not up to her usual standards. Lauren said that she was sorry, but because she had been very busy, she had not put as much effort into this particular assignment.

Mr. Chips waited a couple of days hoping that Lauren would come back and confess that the paper was not hers. When she didn't, Mr. Chips filled out an office discipline referral. Plagiarism was grounds for expulsion from the magnet school. Mr. Chips did not want to see Lauren expelled but he felt compelled to uphold the school's high academic standards.

When Mr. Peabody, the principal, received the referral he turned it over to Ms. Wells, the Dean of Women. Knowing Lauren's background Mr. Peabody asked Ms. Wells to speak to Lauren to try to get her to come clean. If Lauren admitted to plagiarism, perhaps he could impose a less harsh punishment.

When confronted with the evidence against her, Lauren admitted to the plagiarism. The assignment had been to write about a special relationship with a parent. Lauren burst into tears. "I don't have any relationship with either of my parents, never mind a special relationship. I couldn't possibly do that assignment." It took Ms. Wells over an hour to calm Lauren down. When asked why she didn't go to Mr. Chips to ask for an alternate assignment, Lauren said, "I couldn't admit that I didn't have a special relationship with my parents. I felt so guilty, so inferior."

Questions for discussion and reflection:

1. What is the cause for the lack of communication between Lauren and Mr. Chips? Between Lauren and her classmate?

2. Mr. Chips was aware of Lauren's background. Should he have realized that such an assignment would cause problems for her? Could this incident have been prevented?

3. What factors may have caused Lauren to take her classmate's paper and turn it in as her own, especially when the risk of getting caught was so high?

4. How should school officials handle this situation? Should the school's high academic standards take precedence over Lauren's emotional health?

5. What needs to be done to restore Lauren's emotional stability? What can be done to improve communication?

Case Study #5-3

Student: Raymond

Background: Raymond is a third grader who had been adopted as an infant. Not much is known about his early history. His father is a manager for a utility company and his mother works in the school as a teacher's aide. Raymond is an only child.

Raymond is an average student but experiences difficulty in social situations. Raymond tries hard, but just doesn't know how to make friends. Also, he frequently alienates other students by his attempts to be friendly. For example, one day while walking down the hallway Raymond swatted one of his classmates on the behind in what he meant to be a friendly gesture. Unfortunately, the classmate was getting a drink from the bubbler at the time. He didn't think that getting his face soaked was very friendly. Raymond, however, was unable to understand why his classmate was angry with him.

Raymond also has had much difficulty understanding when and how to joke with his peers. His jokes, which are frequently repeats of ones he has heard from adults, can be offensive. For example, Raymond will frequently tell his classmates ethnic jokes and doesn't understand why they are offended. Sometimes his jokes poke fun at characteristics possessed by his classmates. For example, he might joke about an overweight classmate or give him the nickname "Fatso."

Presenting problem: Yesterday, Raymond was playing basketball on the school playground with several other students. Two of the students in the group were black. These two students jokingly referred to each other by using a derogatory ethnic term. Raymond, wanting to join in, addressed the two students using the ethnic slur. Offended, the two students reported the incident to the principal.

The school Raymond attended was proud of the ethnic diversity of its student population. The school was noted for its various cultural and ethnic celebrations throughout the year. The principal was also proud of the fact that the school was relatively free of ethnic incidents. The school has a zero tolerance policy for racial or ethnic discrimination, and in the past students who were involved in such incidents were dealt with harshly.

The principal spoke to Raymond about the incident. Raymond was genuinely confused. He didn't understand why the black students could use that word, but when he used it he was in big trouble. The principal had a dilemma. He was sure that Raymond did not mean to offend, yet the black students were quite offended. He knew he had to take action, but he wanted his action to be appropriate to the situation. To begin he scheduled a conference between Raymond, the two boys, and all of their parents. He wasn't sure where he would go from there.

Questions for discussion and reflection:

1. What type of disciplinary action, if any, would be appropriate in this situation? Why?
2. Raymond is confused about why he can't use a derogatory ethnic term but members of the ethnic group in question are allowed to. Does Raymond have a valid point?
3. What type of ethnic diversity education is called for by this situation? What can be done to foster greater understanding among various ethnic groups?
4. What intervention techniques can be implemented to improve Raymond's social skills?
5. What kinds of communication problems exist in this scenario? What can be done to correct them?

Case Study #5-4

Student: Alan

Background: Alan is a sixth grader who has been placed in a regular education class under the school district's new inclusion policy. Prior to this placement Alan was in a substantially separate class for students who had language based learning disabilities. Due to a speech impediment, Alan also received speech therapy.

Alan's most recent evaluation indicates that he has average intellectual potential but his reading skills are far below grade level. He has excellent math skills but experiences difficulty in all other subjects due to his poor reading skills. His written and expressive language skills are below expectations for his chronological age.

Alan came from an intact family but one that experienced much tragedy. Alan was a twin but his brother had died in infancy of SIDS. An older brother had drowned in a boating accident two years ago. Alan has an older sister and a younger brother.

Alan had always been quite shy and very immature. In fact, he still believed in Santa Claus up through the fifth grade. After his older brother's death, Alan became even more inward. His parents, quite naturally, had become very protective of their remaining children. They had reluctantly agreed to the inclusion plan. In general they were afraid that Alan would fail without the structured support of the special class. However, Alan's teachers explained that the increased exposure to other students would improve his socialization skills. They also felt that he needed exposure to positive role models to assist in his language development.

Alan's inclusion plan called for a special education teacher to consult with his classroom teachers and modify curricular materials. However, all of his instruction was to be provided by the regular education teachers. Provision of a classroom aide was discussed but the pupil personnel team felt that this was not necessary. Alan continued to receive speech therapy twice per week and had one session per week in the resource room with Mrs. Kaye, the special education teacher. The purpose of this weekly session was for the teacher to check in with Alan on a regular basis to make sure all was going well.

Due to his problems with oral language, Alan has difficulty expressing himself. This frequently results in misunderstandings. To compound matters, Alan becomes very nervous when confronted and this impedes his communication skills even more.

Presenting problem: This past week Alan came into the resource room in tears. He was obviously very upset and told the teacher that he didn't want to be in regular education classes any more. He said that the work was too hard and he couldn't do it. Mrs. Kaye was a bit suspicious because she had been in touch with all of his teachers and, although he was below his classmates, they seemed pleased with his overall progress. She questioned him further about his relationships with his teachers. Alan indicated that he liked all of them except for Mr. McLaughlin the social studies teacher. He said that Mr. McLaughlin was real mean. Mrs. Kaye was surprised to hear this because Mr. McLaughlin was one of the best liked teachers in the school. She suspected that there had been a misunderstanding.

Mrs. Kaye approached Mr. McLaughlin during lunch to see if there had been a problem. Mr. McLaughlin stated that Alan had not done his homework the night before. When questioned as to why it was not done, Alan supposedly had said, "Because I had to go bowling." Mr. McLaughlin had made it clear that his homework was more important than bowling. He told Alan that he would have to stay after school to complete the missing assignment. Alan had become very upset about this, completely shut down, and refused to do any of his class assignment. Mr. McLaughlin finally had to call for the vice principal when he was unable to get Alan to cooperate. Mr. McLaughlin explained that he knew he had come down hard on Alan, but that he had been having a problem with homework taking a back seat to little league, dance lessons, gymnastics and other extracurricular activities. Alan going bowling was the last straw. He was quite concerned with what he referred to as Alan's "temper tantrum," stating that perhaps Alan was not mature enough to handle regular education.

Mrs. Kaye was even more confused. Alan's parents were very conscientious and she knew they would not take him bowling before his homework had been completed. She called Alan's mother to try to clear up the story. Alan's mother informed her that he did not go bowling, they had taken him to the Alfred R. Bollen Clinic for an independent evaluation. They had made an afternoon appointment so he would not miss any school and they did not get back until late at night. She said she had given Alan a note explaining this to his teachers. Mrs. Kaye found the note in Alan's backpack.

Mrs. Kaye surmised that the problem was one of miscommunication or misunderstanding. Alan had probably referred to the Bollen Clinic as "Bollen" and when asked why his homework was not completed Alan must have said, "Because I had to go to Bollen." With Alan's speech problem Mr. McLaughlin may have thought he said bowling instead of Bollen. Mr. McLaughlin would not have known what Bollen was.

Questions for discussion and reflection:

1. Was Alan prematurely placed in an inclusionary setting? Should his placement have been more gradual? Were sufficient supports put in place?
2. Knowing that Alan had an expressive language problem, should Mr. McLaughlin have made a greater attempt to get to the bottom of Alan's excuse for not doing his homework?
3. Once confronted with not having done his homework, why was Alan not able to explain that it wasn't his fault?
4. What should now be done to correct the current situation and smooth out Alan's relationship with Mr. McLaughlin?
5. What needs to be done to make sure that something like this doesn't happen again?

Case Study #5-5

Student: Ly

Background: Ly is a 12 year old seventh grader of Asian decent. She has been in the United States for several years now. Initially, Ly received English as a second language instruction but now is quite proficient in English. Ly is an excellent student having made the honor roll the last marking period. Ly does not have much of a social life because she spends so much of her time studying. However, her classmates appear to like and respect her.

Ly's parents place great importance on education and put pressure on her to succeed. They are very hard workers themselves and expect Ly and her two siblings to put forth as much effort as possible in their schoolwork. Her parents' work ethic is such that they do not attend school functions, such as academic awards ceremonies, if these functions conflict with their work schedules. On the surface this appears to be a dichotomy, as one would expect parents who put pressure on their children to succeed in school to attend ceremonies where those children reap the rewards of their efforts. However, the parents also stress that their children must always meet their responsibilities and by fulfilling their job obligations they set an example for their children.

Ly is a very determined young person. She becomes very upset, even angry, when she does not meet her own expectations or those of her parents. For example, Ly is never happy with any grade lower than an A and will become visibly upset if she gets anything less on an assignment.

Presenting problem: At the beginning of the third marking term a student teacher was assigned to Ly's science class. The school was holding a science fair and the student teacher was given the responsibility of assisting students with their projects. Ly selected global warming as the topic for her project. In addition to completing an extensive written report on the effects of global warming she constructed a very detailed diorama to graphically illustrate what could happen to the earth if the problem is not solved.

Ly was very distraught that she did not win the top prize for her grade level. Ly had been given the second place ribbon but was not satisfied with this award. The next day the student teacher tried to console her by telling Ly that what was most important was that she had tried her best. Ly responded, "But my best wasn't good enough, I have to do better." The student teacher was unable to reason with her. Ly was insistent that she had to be the very best and that nothing less was acceptable. When the student teacher asked Ly why it was so important to finish first, Ly could only respond, "Because I have to be the best, that's why." The student teacher was very concerned and wondered whether Ly's parents might be putting too much pressure on her to succeed academically. She couldn't seem to make Ly understand that she had done well and should be proud of her accomplishments.

Later that day the student who had won top prize for the seventh grade found a threatening note in his locker. The note suggested that some physical harm would come to him if he continued to win academic prizes. The note was turned in to the principal who brought it to the attention of the seventh grade teachers to see if they could identify its author. The student teacher was quite sure that it was written by Ly but decided to remain silent and speak with Ly about it herself. As she went home that day she wondered how she could effectively communicate with Ly that although academic success was important, the fact that you did your best was what mattered the most. She also wanted to convey to Ly that success at any price simply wasn't worth it.

Questions for reflection and discussion:

1. The student teacher is unable to communicate to Ly that finishing second is certainly commendable and something she should be proud of. Ly is unable to communicate to the student teacher why it is so important for her to finish first. To what extent is this a problem involving different value systems?

2. The student teacher chose to remain silent when she felt that the note had been written by Ly. Was this a wise decision? Why or why not?

3. What can the student teacher do to establish better two-way communication with Ly? Should she even try? Would it be best to turn to someone else for assistance? If so, who?

4. If the student teacher does speak to Ly about the note herself, how should she approach Ly? What should she do if Ly becomes defensive or hostile?

5. If Ly did write the threatening note, how should this situation be dealt with? Does this call for an immediate disciplinary response? What should be done over the long term?

Chapter 6

Passive-Aggressive Behavior: When the Capable Child Refuses to Conform

In 25 years of teaching Mrs. Kilbride had never encountered a student as frustrating as Billy. It was only the second week of school but he was already driving her crazy. Since entering third grade Billy had not completed a single written assignment, had lost many worksheets, and never seemed to know what was going on when called on during class. Nothing Mrs. Kilbride did seemed to motivate Billy. She had tried positive and negative reinforcements to no avail. She had even resorted to using peer pressure but this had backfired as Billy seemed to do even less when pressured by his classmates. He was not oppositional or defiant. Billy seemed bright enough but he just didn't do anything. She couldn't even get him to complete an assignment when she worked one-on-one with him. He actually seemed to sabotage his own success!

Billy's records indicated that he had been evaluated in the first grade but the team determined that he had "no special needs." During the second grade he was evaluated for attention deficit disorder but those findings also were negative. Billy's second grade teacher could provide no help. She had experienced the same problems and reluctantly admitted that she had "written him off."

Mrs. Kilbride called Billy's mother, Mrs. Thayer. Mrs. Thayer said she had hoped that third grade would be different. She didn't know what to do either and was as frustrated as Mrs. Kilbride. Mrs. Thayer indicated that getting Billy to do his homework was impossible. She said she had given up on punishing him because it didn't do any good. She wondered aloud whether he might be a "head case" that needed to see a psychiatrist. The conversation ended with Mrs. Thayer wishing Mrs. Kilbride "good luck."

Students who are passive-aggressive generally resist the teacher's demands for adequate performance; however the students are generally not outwardly defiant. Rather, their resistance is displayed via procrastination, forgetfulness, or general inefficiency. Students with a passive-aggressive disorder may be dependent on others, lack self-confidence, and even be depressed.

Consequently, students who are passive-aggressive do not make good academic progress. Generally, they perform well below expectations. Frequently, assignments are not completed or are not passed in. Long-term projects are a particular problem for these students. The passive-aggressive student will never refuse to do an assignment. The student just doesn't get around to it, forgets to do it, or loses it altogether.

Passive-aggressive students also have social problems as well. Since they cannot be depended on, their peers tend to avoid working with them. They can be particularly vexing in a cooperative learning situation.

What is particularly frustrating about having a passive-aggressive student in the classroom is that the student never quite connects his or her failures with the behavior. In other words, the student never really takes responsibility for his or her shortcomings.

Behaviorally, passive-aggressive students do not present classroom management problems in the sense that they are not disruptive or dangerous. However, underlying their modus operandi is a pervasive resentment against authority figures. Passive-aggressive students, however, generally do not assert themselves. Thus, although the student's defiance is not overt, it is nonetheless ever-present. In many respects, the fact that the passive-aggressive student does not voice his or her noncompliant stance makes this student particularly frustrating to work with.

To be effective in dealing with a passive-aggressive child, the teacher first needs to recognize that the child is expressing anger in a very inappropriate way. Since many passive-aggressive students have internalized their behavior and may not realize that the teacher is quite aware of what they are doing, it is important to open up lines of communication. The teacher needs to let the student know that what he or she is doing is unproductive and that there will be a consequence of the behavior. For example, the teacher might communicate to a passive-aggressive child, "If you continue to dawdle and don't get that math paper done, you won't be able to go out for recess." This lets the student know that the teacher is aware that the procrastination is intentional and that there will be a logical consequence for it. Most importantly, the teacher should not respond to the passive-aggressive student with an angry outburst. Doing so will only let the child know that he or she has accomplished his or her goal.

Additional Reading

Brophy, J. (1995). Elementary teachers' perceptions of and reported strategies for coping with twelve types of problem students. *ERIC Document Reproduction Service* ED389390.

Bruns, J.H. (1992). They can but they don't: Helping students overcome work inhibition. *American Educator, 16(4)*, 38–47.

Farber, E.W., and Burge-Callaway, K.G. (1988). Differences in anger, hostility, and interpersonal aggressiveness in Type A and Type B adolescents. *ERIC Document Reproduction Service* ED298413.

Gallagher, P.A. (1988). *Teaching Students With Behavior Disorders.* Denver, CO: Love Publishing Co.

Hardt, J. (1988). How passive-aggressive behavior in emotionally disturbed children affects peer interactions in a classroom setting. *ERIC Document Reproduction Service* ED297518.

Killian, C. (1994). The passive-aggressive paradox of on-line discourse. *Technos, 3(2),* 18–19.

Newcomer, P.L. (1993). *Understanding and Teaching Emotionally Disturbed Children and Youth.* Austin, TX: Pro-Ed.

Schwartz, D. (1993). Antecedents of aggression and peer victimization: A prospective study. *ERIC Document Reproduction Service* ED356886.

Sherman, R. (1994). Defusing the power play by playing inadequate, playing good. *Family Journal, 2(2),* 158–162.

Case Studies

Case Study #6-1

Student: Carlos

Background: Carlos is the only child of European immigrants. He is currently a second grader who receives English as a Second Language services. The family has been in the United States for four years. Carlos' father works in a restaurant and his mother is unemployed although she occasionally babysits. Carlos also receives speech therapy for a stammer. Carlos' parents, particularly his father, claim to be very strict with him. The family is very religious.

Carlos has done quite well academically; however, his teachers have noticed that he frequently doesn't do assignments that he doesn't want to do. His first grade teacher felt that he was unable to do these assignments because of his limited English proficiency. His second grade teacher has noted, however, that Carlos doesn't understand what Carlos chooses not to understand. Carlos never balks at doing an assignment, he just doesn't do it. When questioned about why an assignment isn't completed Carlos generally cries and says that it was too hard. Sometimes papers are lost and even his reading workbook disappeared. It was later found by the custodian in the bathroom waste basket.

Presenting problem: The more serious problem is that Carlos has been stealing. His mother was the first to become aware of the problem when she found several cassette tapes in his backpack. Thinking that they might belong to the school, she brought them to his teacher. Carlos was disciplined by the school for taking the tapes. Carlos' teacher felt that it was an isolated incident and that it wouldn't happen again. She was wrong. Several days later Carlos was caught taking computer disks from the school's library. Carlos was placed on an in-school suspension for this second offense. While in the vice principal's office Carlos stole several pens from the V.P.'s desk. When confronted with the thefts, even when caught with the merchandise, Carlos denied that he took anything. He always claimed that someone gave the things to him but could never say who.

School officials had a conference with Carlos' mother. She was urged to take Carlos for counseling but resisted saying, "We can take care of this ourselves." After a few more incidents of stealing school officials suggested that a conference with Carlos' father should be set up. Carlos' mother explained that she had not told her husband about Carlos' stealing because he was very strict and would hit Carlos. She begged school officials to not inform her husband and seemed to be genuinely afraid of what he might do. Counseling was brought up again but Carlos' mother again rejected the idea saying, "We don't tell other people our problems." Eventually, she agreed to talk to her priest about the matter.

Carlos' mother says she doesn't understand why he is stealing and insists that she has punished him for his transgressions. However, school officials feel that she is not as strict as she claims to be. On the afternoon following a school conference called because of one of Carlos' incidents of thefts, the school's secretary saw Carlos' mother in a toy store buying him a small toy for being "such a good boy."

At this point, the school is in a quandary. School personnel feel that Carlos has a serious problem that will only get worse if it is not addressed. However, they don't think that continued discipline is the answer.

Questions for reflection and discussion:

1. To what extent is Carlos' stealing a reflection of his passive-aggressive behavior?
2. Is the school correct that continued discipline will not solve Carlos' problem? Since his mother is not agreeable to counseling, what can be done?
3. In spite of his mother's concerns, should Carlos' father be appraised of the situation? Do school officials have the right, and/or responsibility to inform him in spite of the mother's objections. What responsibility would school officials have if Carlos' father hurt him?
4. To what extent is Carlos' mother part of the problem?
5. What strategies, short of a daily shakedown, can school personnel employ to deal with Carlos' stealing?

Case Study #6-2

Student: Isaac

Background: Isaac is a fairly bright 10 year old fourth grader attending an elementary school in a middle class community. He lives with his parents and five siblings: an older sister, an older brother, two younger sisters, and a younger brother. Isaac's parents are both professionals: his mother is the office manager of a medical clinic and his father is a chemical engineer. On recent standardized achievement tests, Isaac scored above the 90th percentile in reading and math. His score on a group intelligence test was 137. These scores would normally qualify Isaac for the school district's gifted and talented program which begins in grade five. However, Isaac's teacher, Mrs. Cassidy, will not provide him with a recommendation for this program because of his poor work habits. Without his teacher's recommendation it is unlikely that he will be accepted into the program. Quite frankly, Mrs. Cassidy was surprised that he scored so high because he had never shown that kind of ability in class.

Isaac is a very large boy who enjoys sports and games. He loves to play kickball during recess. The other students frequently complain that Isaac "cheats" and makes up new rules as the game goes along. When the game is closely watched by a staff member, Isaac appears to be playing by the rules. However, as soon as the staff member leaves the kickball field to supervise another part of the playground, the complaints about Isaac begin.

Similar problems exist in the classroom regarding assignments. If Isaac is closely supervised, his assignments are completed and passed in. However, when he is allowed to work on his own, assignments are not always passed in. When questioned about the whereabouts of a missing assignment, Isaac will insist that he turned it in. Long term projects are a disaster. During the second half of the year the class worked on state reports. Each student was required to choose a state, gather information about that state, and write a report. This required library research along with some independent research such as writing to various bureaus within the state for information. Although Isaac worked on his report during class time, he never completed it. Mrs. Cassidy held several conferences with him to check on his progress to no avail. Isaac lost research notes and misplaced information he had received from the state bureaus. He insisted that someone stole the map he had drawn of his state.

As might be expected, Isaac also has difficulty working in cooperative learning situations. Other students complain that he doesn't do his fair share of the work and that all he does is copy what they've done. When Mrs. Cassidy speaks to him about these complaints, Isaac puts the blame for the problems on the other students saying that they don't like him and won't take any of his suggestions. Regarding the comments that he just copies, Isaac says the other students are lying.

Presenting problem: When Isaac's mother found out that his teacher would not be recommending him for the gifted and talented program she went to see the principal, Mr. Santos. She complained to the principal that Isaac was being picked on by his teacher who never gave him any credit for his accomplishments. She couldn't understand how the teacher could not recommend someone as smart as Isaac for the program. She deduced that Mrs. Cassidy didn't like Isaac and just wasn't being fair. As if to prove her point, she said that she couldn't understand how a teacher could give a student with Isaac's test scores only B's and C's on his report card.

Mr. Santos called Mrs. Cassidy down to the office to speak with Isaac's mother. Mrs. Cassidy explained that the gifted and talented program required self-initiative, task commitment, and organizational skills that she felt Isaac simply did not have. She gave the example of the state report explaining that this report was a very basic task compared to what would be required in the gifted and talented program. She stated that she could not recommend a student for this program who could not work independently.

Isaac's mother said that she felt that Isaac had not been challenged in Mrs. Cassidy's class and was bored. She felt that he would rise to the occasion if he was placed in the gifted and talented program. She stated that she thought he should be given the opportunity.

Mrs. Cassidy explained that she could not recommend a student that she felt was not gifted and talented program material. She opined that if she recommended him and he failed, that future recommendations from her would not carry much weight. She stated that she would not be willing to put her reputation at risk.

When Isaac's mother commented that she was unaware that he was having any problems getting his work done, Mrs. Cassidy reminded her that she had failed to come in for two scheduled parent-teacher conferences. At that Isaac's mother retorted, "Well I'm busy. After all I work eight hours a day, not six like you teachers."

Mr. Santos stated that he felt Mrs. Cassidy was justified in not recommending Isaac for the gifted and talented program. Isaac's mother angrily left the meeting stating that she was going to call the school board chairperson who was a personal friend of hers. Her final words were, "You'll be sorry you ever messed with me."

Questions for reflection and discussion:

1. What could be the underlying causes of Isaac's failure to complete assignments when he obviously has the intellectual capacity to do well?

2. What steps could Mrs. Cassidy have taken earlier in the school year to address Isaac's lack of initiative and inability to work independently?
3. How are Isaac's classroom behaviors and playground behaviors similar? How are they different?
4. Could Isaac's mother be correct that he is bored in Mrs. Cassidy's class and will rise to the challenge of the gifted and talented program? Should he be given the opportunity? Is Mrs. Cassidy justified in not recommending him?
5. Do Isaac's mother's behavior and attitudes contribute to his passive-aggressive personality style?

Case Study #6-3

Student: Sean

Background: Sean is a 13 year old student in the sixth grade at the Raven Elementary School. Sean has mixed ancestry as his father is white and his mother is Native American. His parents met while his father was in the military. When Sean was two years old his father deserted the family following an overseas tour of duty. There has been no contact with him since then, although Sean's mother did receive support while he was still in the military. Sean's mother works as a floor supervisor in a garment factory.

Sean repeated the second and fourth grades because of academic difficulties, particularly in reading and math. Much of his academic difficulty is attributed to excessive absenteeism. Some years he has been absent without a valid excuse up to 40% of the time. His mother has always made excuses for his absences stating that he is sick, but has never produced a doctor's note when requested. School officials suspect that she is very lenient with Sean and allows him to do as he pleases. He is known to the local police who have frequently taken him home when they have found him in places that are known to be havens for drifters, vandals, and drug addicts. The police don't consider him to be a serious problem, but rather think of him more as a nuisance. In fact they note that he is always polite and respectful. They do, however, regard his mother as being strange and aloof. Recently they have noted that she seems to have a new boyfriend who is much younger. When found together they generally appear to have been drinking. The boyfriend has a court record for minor offenses.

Sean's school performance is rather inconsistent. His skills are fragmented and splintered, most likely as a result of his sporadic attendance pattern. His word attack skills are adequate but he comprehends very little. He scores at an average level for his grade on standardized math tests but generally does poorly on daily assignments. His teachers feel that this is due to carelessness on his part. They feel that he is not interested in academics and hasn't assumed responsibility for his own success or failure. They consider him to be cooperative until demands are placed on him. For instance, although he seldom shows overt agitation or anger, he seems to have the ability to ruin a classroom climate of cooperation. During these times Sean looks on with a rather curious smirk on his face but has not done anything noticeably inappropriate.

Sean's sixth grade teacher, Mrs. Carrol, is a relatively young teacher who believes that every student can and must experience success and that it is her job to make sure that each one does succeed. She has worked with Sean on prosocial skills such as listening to others, asking for help when needed, and making appropriate decisions. Sean has responded well to her efforts and has made an attempt toward adding to the classroom environment rather than subtracting from it. Mrs. Carroll feels that she has made progress with Sean.

Mrs. Carrol recently introduced a new language arts activity in an attempt to encourage more spontaneity among class members in verbal exchanges. During exchanges between class members students are at liberty to discuss any aspect of their personal lives they wish to share. The interpersonal exchanges are generally informal to encourage more open peer conversation. If students wish, they may talk to Mrs. Carrol during these times.

Presenting problem: In monitoring the peer conversations Mrs. Carrol has sensed a certain uneasiness among the students. Privately, some students have indicated that Sean makes it difficult for others to speak because of his need to speak. When questioned these students have stated that Sean's stories are scary and weird. They reported that he speaks about scary things that his mother and boyfriend do on weekends and he claims that when he is older he will take part in these activities. One of the students even confided in Mrs. Carrol that she has nightmares about some of Sean's stories.

Mrs. Carrol decided to speak with Sean to see if she could get a handle on why the students were so concerned. When Mrs. Carrol told him what she already knew, Sean just smiled but said very little. Mrs. Carrol felt resistance when she tried to prompt Sean to be more open with her. Finally, in desperation Mrs. Carrol told Sean that she felt it was necessary to schedule a meeting with his mother. At that, Sean's smirk became even more frightening but he still said nothing.

Mrs. Carrol met with Sean's mother, the boyfriend, and Sean the following week. The conference was difficult as Sean's mother initially came on strong demanding to know what the problem was. Mrs. Carrol could not find a diplomatic way to express her concerns and finally blurted out, "Please don't take offense, but is there anything you do on weekends that would be upsetting to children." She explained about the stories Sean had told that had frightened the other children. The boyfriend started to laugh uneasily.

After a long silence Sean's mother related that since she and her boyfriend don't have a lot of money they have taken up rat shooting as a sport. Apparently they buy a couple of six packs of beer and go to an abandoned factory and shoot the rats with a 22 rifle. She took pride in stating that she was a good shot. Sean had been told that when he was older he could accompany them but that he would have to buy his own beer.

Mrs. Carrol thanked them for coming and said that she better understood the situation. She decided to meet privately with Sean the next day to try to bring closure to the situation.

Questions for discussion and reflection:

1. Does the rat shooting incident help to explain Sean's passive-aggressive behavior? How?
2. What should Mrs. Carrol say to Sean when she meets with him tomorrow? Why? What should she say to the class?
3. Should Mrs. Carrol continue with her new language arts activity? Why or why not?
4. Do you think Mrs. Carrol has a better understanding of Sean's needs as a result of her conference with his mother and boyfriend? How should she react? What are the long-term implications for Sean's behavior? How should Mrs. Carrol respond to Sean in the future?
5. Should Mrs. Carrol relay this story to another professional? Who should she seek out for assistance in dealing with Sean?

Case Study #6-4

Student: Ralph

Background: Ralph is a sophomore attending a large comprehensive high school in an affluent suburb. He lives with his maternal grandmother. When Ralph was in the seventh grade his mother died of a drug overdose. At the time it was suspected that her death could have been a suicide although that could not be confirmed because she did not leave a note. She had been a drug addict for some time so it is possible that her overdose was accidental. Ralph's father lives nearby in a homeless shelter. Ralph does not have regular contact with him but does see him occasionally picking up bottles and cans along the roadway.

Ralph is a bright youngster but is not overly ambitious. In class he is very lethargic and difficult to motivate. He shows little interest in his schoolwork or in completing assignments. Generally, he does the bare minimum necessary to get by. Overall, he maintains a C average but his teachers feel that he could do much better. He has been seeing a therapist since his mother's death. The therapist does not feel that he is clinically depressed although around the annual anniversary of his mother's death he does become quite sad. He has been diagnosed as having a passive-aggressive personality with oppositional tendencies.

Ralph's grandmother seems to be overwhelmed with the responsibility of caring for him. She works full-time in an office. Her other children are all grown and living on their own. She has stated that at this point in her life she did not expect to be saddled with a child but Ralph is her "flesh and blood" so she feels responsible for caring for him. She pretty much lets him come and go as he pleases. Fortunately, Ralph is basically a good kid and does not get into any trouble in spite of the lack of guidance he receives.

Ralph has a few friends but no one that he calls his "best friend." He has few interests except for playing video games and basketball. He enjoys being part of a pick-up game but does not play on the school's basketball team. He tried out as a freshman and made the team but quit after a few weeks. He had difficulty getting to practice on time (even though it was held right after school) and missed the bus for the first two away games. When the coach spoke to him about his tardiness, Ralph quit. Earlier this year he joined the chess club but soon lost interest and stopped going. He had a part-time job bagging groceries after school but was fired for coming in late too often.

Presenting problem: On the last anniversary of his mother's death, one of Ralph's friends told the guidance counselor that Ralph was talking about committing suicide. The counselor spoke with Ralph and completed a suicide evaluation. She determined that he was not serious about killing himself but felt that his threat should be taken seriously. She contacted his grandmother and told her that Ralph needed to be taken to his therapist immediately. Ralph's grandmother resisted saying she didn't have time. She reluctantly agreed when the counselor threatened to contact the Department of Social Services. However, it was obvious that she was annoyed.

After speaking to Ralph the therapist agreed that there was no danger that he would kill himself but felt that his threats were a cry for help. She felt that Ralph needed more structure in his life and informed his grandmother that she needed to play a more active parenting role. At that Ralph's grandmother became upset, stating that she was doing the best she could. She added that if what she was doing wasn't good enough, then perhaps Ralph should be placed in a foster home. Ralph overheard this comment.

Since this episode, Ralph's grades have gone downhill. He is in danger of failing the last quarter. He is not doing any homework and does very little in class. He often comes to class and just puts his head down on his desk. When his teachers try to talk to him about his failure to complete work he tells them he'll try to do better. He might improve for a day or two, but there has been no long term improvement. The counselor told Ralph that he might have to go to summer school if he failed the last quarter. Ralph thought that summer school might be a good idea because he was usually bored during the summer. At this point the staff is very frustrated. His teachers don't know how to motivate him and are afraid of losing him completely. One teacher has even suggested that perhaps a residential school for emotionally disturbed adolescents might be appropriate.

Questions for reflection and discussion:

1. What can be the cause of Ralph's apparent lack of energy and lethargic demeanor? How could this have been better addressed in the past?
2. Ralph appears to be bright but is an underachiever. What is the cause of his lack of interest in school? How does his family situation contribute to his failure to work up to his ability level?
3. What steps could Ralph's teachers take to better motivate him and help him reach his potential as a student?
4. What can be done to help Ralph develop other extracurricular interests? If an interest is developed, what can be done to help him stick with it?
5. Has Ralph reached the point where he needs a residential school as suggested by one of his teachers?

Case Study #6-5

Student: Andy

Background: Andy is a ten year old fifth grader who lives with his grandmother. Andy's mother is a drug addict who abandoned him many years ago. He has lived with his grandmother since he was an infant. His mother currently lives on the streets and in homeless shelters. She sporadically surfaces at the grandmother's house, generally looking for money. His father's whereabouts are unknown but it is felt that he has left the country and has returned to his homeland. Andy's grandmother is illiterate. She has never been able to hold down a job for very long but is currently enrolled in an adult literacy program.

Andy received resource room support for reading in the first, second and third grades. Testing indicates that he has average intelligence and does not have any learning disabilities. He was terminated from the resource room program because the evaluation team felt that he was very capable of performing at grade level and that his failure to do so was caused by a lack of motivation, not an inability to do the work. It was also felt that he performed no better with the resource room support. Andy historically has not been overly ambitious. He does not complete any homework assignments and rarely completes written work in the classroom. He has been evaluated for attention deficit disorder but all these assessments were negative. Andy's teachers have tried everything to motivate him to no avail, including positive reinforcements, negative reinforcements, and outright punishment. Andy has never been retained because it is felt that it would do no good. The school has tried to work with his grandmother to improve his motivation but she has never followed through on any agreements made with Andy's teachers. For example he was once put on a daily progress report that his grandmother was supposed to review and sign. (Recognizing that she was illiterate, the school devised a simple progress report that used symbols instead of a narrative.) After a couple of days she stopped signing the reports.

Andy has never been a behavior problem in school. In fact his teachers often joked that he was too lazy to even misbehave. Recently, however, he has been getting into serious trouble with juvenile authorities. The summer before he started the fifth grade he broke into a neighbor's house and stole some cash and bullets. Thus far during the school year the juvenile detective has arrested him for shoplifting from a local convenience store, breaking the windshield on a neighbor's car, and stealing candy bars from younger children who were selling them to raise money for a scout troop. In each case the charges were filed but no punitive action was taken. The juvenile court ordered his grandmother to take him to counseling. She took him for two sessions but then stopped. In spite of these incidents, Andy has still not been a behavior problem in school.

Presenting problem: Mrs. Naughton, a neighbor of Andy's came to the school one morning and asked to see the principal right away. She was very agitated. She told the principal that the previous afternoon she had found Andy in bed fondling her first grade son. Each was partially disrobed. When she questioned her son he indicated that Andy had threatened to beat him up if he didn't do what Andy told him to do. He also confessed that this was not the first time it had happened. Mrs. Naughton reported the incident to the juvenile detective and also filed a petition with the Department of Social Services complaining that Andy's grandmother was not capable of properly supervising him. She asked the principal to make sure that Andy did not have any contact with her son during the school day.

A few hours later Andy's grandmother came to the school and asked to speak to the counselor. She complained that Mrs. Naughton was spreading lies about Andy and denied that the alleged incident ever happened. She sobbed as she informed the counselor that the Department of Social

Most changes that have taken place have come from outside the profession itself and were dictated by individuals who have not had first hand classroom teaching experiences. Advice about classroom management practices from psychologists is just one example of such external influence.

Thus when students' basic needs and supplies are denied for any reason and symptom choice is internalized the seeds of personalized conflict result. The inability or failure of immediate adult authorities to effectively intervene, lead to the individual developing feelings of inadequacy with regard to self-management responsibility. Unless the adults in attendance respond quickly to such circumstances to provide the correct dosages of what is needed, the individual retreats further and further away from external help and learns to depend upon his/her own behavior in navigating life space experiences. This group of behavior problems represent a formidable challenge to all socially conscious adults.

Additional Reading

Abbott, S. (1993). Growing up in an alcoholic family. *Journal of Emotional and Behavioral Problems, 2(3)*, 8–10.

Charles, C.M. (1992). *Building Classroom Discipline* (4th Ed.). White Plains, NY: Longman.

Cruz, M.H., and DeLamarter, W.A. (1988). Victim sex, personal similarity, and victim behavior: A case of violated expectations. *ERIC Document Reproduction Service* ED301780.

Gemmill, G. (1989). The dynamics of scapegoating in small groups. *Small Group Behavior, 20(4)*, 406–418.

Nolan, M.J. et al. (1995). Student victimization at school: Statistics in brief. *ERIC Document Reproduction Service* ED388439.

Rexford, E. (1976). An American mythology: We care for our children. Keynote Address: Second Child Advocacy Conference. Durham, NH: New England Child Mental Health Task Force.

Schwartz, D. (1993). Antecedents of aggression and peer victimization: A prospective study. *ERIC Document Reproduction Service* ED356886.

Webb, W. (1993). Cognitive behavior therapy with children of alcoholics. *School Counselor, 40(3)*, 170–177.

White, J.W., and Humphrey, J.A. (1995). Victimization status and perceived risk of sexual assault: Longitudinal analyses. *ERIC Document Reproduction Service* ED393041.

White, J.W,. and Humphrey, J.A. (1993). Sexual revictimization: A longitudinal perspective. *ERIC Document Reproduction Service* ED374363.

Wilczenski, F.L. et al. (1994). Promoting "fair play": Interventions for children as victims and victimizers. *ERIC Document Reproduction Service* 380744.

Case Studies

Case Study #7-1

Student: Wayne

Background: Wayne is a slightly built ninth grader attending a comprehensive high school. Wayne has always been an outcast among his peers and does not have a single close friend. He has always suffered ridicule because of one of his most prominent features — his large ears. He also has other physical features, such as large teeth and close set eyes, that make him physically unattractive.

Wayne has never shown any inclination for athletics and, in fact, is very uncoordinated. As a result he is often picked on by other students who bump into him, push him, etc. Wayne will never retaliate and as a result suffers much physical abuse at the hands of other students. When he was in the middle school his teachers and counselors were very concerned that Wayne was always the victim of other students' pranks. However, except for meting out discipline to the pranksters when caught, little was done to address the situation.

Wayne is, however, very capable academically. In particular he has always excelled in math and science. Since entering the high school he has taken an active interest in computers and has even built his own computer. His teachers have been amazed at his ability to program and feel he definitely has a future in this area.

Wayne's father is a Viet Nam war veteran and is very active in veteran's organizations. He has expressed disappointment that Wayne is such a "coward" and "wimp." He had hoped that Wayne would choose a career in the military and is disappointed that this is unlikely to happen. Wayne's older sister Betty has, however, expressed an interest in the military. She is looking into joining the R.O.T.C. and possibly attending a military college. Their father often jokes that Betty is the son he always wanted. Wayne is very aware of his father's disappointment but does not like to talk about it.

Wayne has never been a discipline problem. Rather, the problem has been how other students have treated him. On a few occasions Wayne has been physically hurt by other students. However, when school officials attempt to discipline the other students, Wayne refuses to testify against them.

Presenting problem: For several weeks Wayne had been telling his math teacher that someday he'd do something that would make the other kids respect him. That someday came two days ago when Wayne successfully entered the school's computer system and altered the report card grades of all ninth grade students. The students were overjoyed when they received report cards with all A's. However, school officials were not overjoyed. In fact, they are no longer impressed with his computer skills.

When confronted, Wayne readily, and proudly, admitted that he was the one who altered the grades. In fact, he told the principal that he could design a better computer security system for the school. For his efforts, Wayne was suspended for 10 days. The school is considering filing criminal charges.

Questions for reflection and discussion:

1. What are the factors that may have led Wayne to commit this act of sabotage?
2. School officials have known that Wayne is the victim of abuse from other students for some time. In addition to taking disciplinary action against the other students, what could school officials have done to deal with this situation?
3. Is the 10 day suspension justified? Would another disciplinary sanction have been more appropriate?
4. Is the principal justified in filing criminal charges? Why or why not?
5. Should the school take Wayne up on his offer to design a better computer security system?
6. Wayne has three more years in the high school. What must be done in the future to deal with Wayne's low self-esteem?

Case Study #7-2

Student: Greg

Background: Greg is a nine year old third grader who recently enrolled in a public school. He had previously attended a parochial school. A few days into the school year Greg's teacher contacted his mother because she had some concerns about his behavior. Greg's mother confided that he had been repeatedly sexually abused by his father and had a history of sexually abusing other boys. In fact, he had basically been expelled from the parochial school because he had abused several of his classmates. Greg's mother was quite open about his history and gave the school permission to contact his therapist.

Initially, Greg had been allowed to see his father only if the visit was supervised by a court appointed monitor. However, since many of the incidents of sexual activity occurred immediately after these supervised visits, they were also curtailed. Thus, Greg no longer has any contact with his father. However, the sexual incidents have continued sporadically.

Greg's teacher has found that he has difficulty interacting with his classmates. Greg is very demanding and always wants his own way. If the other children don't go along with what he wants, he won't have anything to do with them. On several occasions Greg has made caustic remarks to his classmates. When told to apologize he will do so half-heartedly. His teacher is very concerned about his mean streak and his lack of concern when he hurts another child's feelings. In fact Greg sometimes thinks its a joke. For example, one day after Greg told another student that she was stupid the teacher told him to tell Carol he was sorry. Greg's response was, "I'm sorry you're stupid."

Presenting problem: The day after the meeting with Greg's mother, Mrs. Kramer, the school's guidance counselor, called Greg's therapist, Mr. Reeves. Mr. Reeves stated emphatically that Greg should never be allowed to be alone with another boy, especially a younger boy. He indicated that Greg's activities with other boys included sexual talk, getting them to pull down their pants, and sexual touching. Mr. Reeves felt that Greg presented a threat to other children unless he was very closely supervised. Mr. Reeves indicated that Greg should never be out of sight of an adult supervisor and shouldn't even be allowed to engage in conversation with another boy unless an adult was within hearing distance because of the possibility of sexual talk. Apparently Greg can be very dominant and has the ability to persuade other boys to go along with his "plans." He is also able to convince them that they should never "tell" an adult what they have done. Greg has not shown any interest in girls thus far.

The school immediately implemented the following precautions: Greg's teacher would take the class to the rest rooms twice daily and, after determining that the boys' room was vacant would allow the boys to use it one at a time; if Greg needed to go at other times his teacher would notify the office with a prearranged code so that a male administrator could immediately go supervise the rest room; Greg would be closely supervised at lunch and recess by the vice principal, Greg would not be paired with or seated near any boys for instruction or class activities; Greg's desk would be located as close to the teacher's as possible without making it obvious; and all special subject teachers who had contact with Greg would be notified of these precautions.

The superintendent was informed of the situation and the implemented precautionary procedures. He immediately notified the school board attorney and requested advice. He also authorized the school to hire a male aide to supervise Greg at all times. In addition, he advised the special education director to conduct a complete evaluation to determine if Greg qualified as disabled, and if so, to determine if another placement would better meet his needs?

Questions for discussion and reflection:

1. What responsibility does the school have to protect other students in the school from Greg? How can school officials balance the rights of other students with Greg's rights? Whose rights should take precedence?

2. Does the school district have a responsibility to notify the parents of other students of the potential threat Greg poses? How does this square with Greg's confidentiality rights? Again, whose rights take precedence?

3. Do school officials have any responsibility to notify the parents of children Greg may encounter in the neighborhood of Greg's past history?

4. Are the precautions the school has implemented reasonable? Should any other precautions be implemented?

5. Is the superintendent's authorization to hire a male aide a rational step or is it one that is not necessary?

6. Are the superintendent's instructions to the special education administrator valid or do they infringe on Greg rights to an education in the least restrictive environment?

7. What questions should be asked of the school board attorney?

Case Study #7-3

Student: Jennifer

Background: Jennifer is a second grader who has been repeatedly sexually abused by her father who is a drug addict. Jennifer lives with her mother and younger sister, Jessica, who was also abused. Their father, by court order, is only allowed supervised visits with the children. However, he has not visited them in over a year. Their mother, Mrs. Baker, works at a local hospital as a nurse's aide.

Both girls have been actively involved in therapy for a little over a year. The abuse incidents were first discovered when Jennifer was in kindergarten and her teacher noticed that she engaged in sexual play and sexual talk with boys in the class. At that time Jennifer attended a private school. Concerned about her behavior, the teacher brought the matter to the attention of the principal. The principal notified the Department of Children and Youth Services who conducted an investigation. Although Jennifer's father denied all allegations, there was considerable evidence against him. In fact the social worker conducting the investigation reported that his behavior toward her during an interview was highly inappropriate. Apparently, he made suggestive comments to the interviewer.

Jennifer enrolled in a public school for the first grade. The school was not informed of her background. Within a few weeks problems developed. Her teacher noticed that Jennifer seemed to prefer the company of boys rather than girls. During free time or recess she was often found in a remote area of the classroom or playground alone with one of the boys in the class. When this was brought to Mrs. Baker's attention during a report card conference, Mrs. Baker filled the teacher in on Jennifer's background. The teacher passed the information on to the principal and guidance counselor. It was decided that everyone needed to keep a close eye on Jennifer but that she should not be treated like a prisoner.

The teacher became very concerned one day when she went to the school's cafeteria before the lunch period had ended. She found Jennifer with her head buried in a boy's lap. The boy seemed to be unaware of what Jennifer was doing. Jennifer initially said that she was just resting her head, but on further questioning stated that she was kissing the boy's penis.

An investigation revealed that Jennifer had engaged in sexual conduct with at least six boys in her first grade classroom and four others in her neighborhood. Most of this sexual conduct involved showing and touching intimate parts of their anatomy. Jennifer had told each of the boys that they shouldn't tell anyone about the activity because they would get into big trouble.

An emergency meeting was held that included Jennifer's therapist as well as school officials. The therapist indicated that he was quite concerned about Jennifer because she did not seem to have any impulse control. She seemed to understand that the sexual behavior was inappropriate; but was very compulsive and could not control her urges. He stated that for the safety of other students, it was necessary that Jennifer be supervised at all times. It was agreed by all that Jennifer should be home tutored for the remainder of the year. Mrs. Baker, alarmed by what had transpired, was in full agreement. In fact, Mrs. Baker even stated that she would consent to a residential placement if school officials thought that this was best and would be willing to pay for it.

Presenting problem: As can be imagined the parents of the students involved in the first grade incidents were alarmed. Due to pressure from those parents, Jennifer was transferred to another school within the district for the second grade. A classroom aide was also provided to basically shadow Jennifer throughout the school day. This was done primarily for the protection of other students.

Jennifer's classroom teacher and special subject teachers who would have contact with her were informed about her past history. However, others in the school were not given that information as it was considered confidential. It was explained to other staff members that the aide was being provided in accordance with Jennifer's Individualized Education Plan (IEP). This was not accurate, however, as Jennifer was not a special education student and did not have an IEP.

All seemed to go well for several months. However, one day the aide was out sick and a replacement could not be found. During recess that day the teacher on duty (who was unaware of Jennifer's background) found Jennifer and a male student hiding behind the school's dumpster. Jennifer had her hand in the boy's pants. An emergency conference was called to discuss the situation. Among the agenda items will be consideration for removing her from the general education environment.

Questions for discussion and reflection:

1. After having been a victim of sexual abuse, what has caused Jennifer to now abuse others? Was this pattern predictable?
2. What factors contributed to the latest sexual incident? How could this have been prevented?
3. Of paramount concern is the safety of other students. Is it necessary to remove Jennifer from the general education environment to protect the safety of others?
4. If Jennifer is removed from the general education environment, what type of educational placement would be appropriate? Who should pay for it?
5. What other services or therapeutic interventions are needed here?
6. There are a number of other difficult issues involved in a situation such as this. Are Jennifer's confidentiality and privacy rights more important than the rights of other students to attend school without being abused? Does the school have a responsibility to inform the parents of others with whom Jennifer comes in contact (i.e. in after school activities) of the danger to their children?
7. Mrs. Baker has been quite cooperative. What if she had not been? Could school officials justify home tutoring Jennifer or otherwise removing her from the general education environment?

Case Study #7-4

Student: Jerry

Background: Jerry is a four year old youngster attending an integrated preschool special education program. Jerry is not one of the special education students, but is one of the nondisabled students placed in the class to provide positive role models. Jerry is an only child who lives with both parents. They wanted him in this program because they felt he needed to develop better socialization skills before entering kindergarten. He was selected for the program by lottery.

Jerry's mother appears to be very shy. She speaks only if spoken to and even then is hesitant and does not make eye contact. The school's staff feels that she may be somewhat limited intellectually. She is not very attractive, having a general waif-like, emaciated appearance. She does not work outside the home.

Jerry's father, on the other hand, is very outgoing and assertive. He is a very well-dressed, distinguished man who appears to be athletic. He is a manager at a local manufacturing plant and is very active in his church. Those who work for him at the plant say he is a perfectionist and can become very angry if tasks are not completed according to his expectations. Overall, he has a controlling, aggressive personality.

Jerry tends to be more like his mother. He appears to be shy, even timid. He does not mix well with other children and backs off quickly when others become aggressive. Jerry cries easily, especially when he feels threatened. Jerry is easily taken advantage of by other children. For example, when playing with other students he does not protest if they take toys away from him. Jerry will simply go get another toy.

Presenting problem: Since he entered the program the staff has noticed that Jerry comes to school with an unusual number of bruises. When questioned about these bruises his mother explained that he was clumsy and fell often. In school, however, he was not clumsy and hardly ever fell. Jerry never verbalized how he received the bruises and, in fact, seemed to become frightened when questioned about them.

The staff became extremely concerned when Jerry came to school with what appeared to be a human bite mark. Again, Jerry seemed unwilling or unable to explain how he got the bite mark. When confronted with this latest incident, his mother stated that Jerry's cousin had bitten him while they were playing. The school nurse, however, determined that the mark was too large to be from a child. She filed an abuse and neglect petition with the Department of Social Services.

When Jerry's father found out that the nurse had filed the abuse and neglect petition, he was enraged. He called the nurse and told her that she needed to start minding her own business and should not be meddling in other people's affairs. He threatened to sue her for defamation of character. When the nurse informed him that she was a mandated reporter and was required by state law to file the report, he retorted, "Well, if you want to discuss what's legal you'll hear from my attorney. I hope you've got a good bank account because I'm going to sue you for everything you own." He then slammed the telephone down. Jerry hasn't been in school since.

Questions for discussion and reflection:

1. Is Jerry's overall demeanor consistent with a child who has been abused? What about his mother, is it possible that she is being abused?
2. If Jerry is being abused, who is the likely abuser, his father or his mother?
3. If the Department of Social Services determines that physical abuse occurred, what family services should be offered? Should punitive action be taken?
4. What are the educational implications for Jerry? What does he require in terms of educational strategies and therapeutic interventions? What can be done to improve his socialization skills?
5. If the abuse and neglect petition is not substantiated, what can the school's staff do to mend the relationship with Jerry's parents?

Case Study #7-5

Student: Shirley

Background: Shirley is a 13 year old sixth grader who repeated the first grade due to learning problems. Shirley has an assessed I.Q. of 65, but through extraordinary effort has managed to succeed in a regular education classroom with resource room support. In fact, her teachers have always been amazed at how well she has done academically in spite of her cognitive limitations.

Shirley is the oldest of five children. She was conceived when her mother was raped at the age of 17. The rapist was never caught. Shirley has one younger sister and three younger brothers. These four children have two different fathers. Shirley's mother, Mrs. Rolph, is married to the father of the youngest two children. Unfortunately, Mr. Rolph is an alcoholic who is in and out of a rehabilitation center.

As the oldest child Shirley has had much responsibility for her younger siblings. However, that is a responsibility that she has borne well. Since Mrs. Rolph works nights, Shirley has had to get supper for the family, make sure the younger siblings finished their homework, and put them to bed. She is also responsible for getting them up in the morning, getting their breakfast, and getting them off to school. In many respects Shirley acts like their mother rather than their sister. In fact the youngest brother often refers to her as his mother. Shirley even stops in at their elementary school from time to time to see how they are doing.

Presenting problem: Suddenly, Shirley's academic achievement took a nose-dive. She began to fail all her subjects and stopped bringing in her homework on a regular basis. Shirley had always been a quiet girl but she became even quieter. Her teachers noted that she seemed to be sad, almost depressed about something. When one teacher asked why she was not bringing in her homework, Shirley just shrugged but tears appeared in her eyes.

A telephone call to the elementary school her younger siblings attended revealed that the younger children did not seem to be as well cared for. It was reported that lately they had been coming to school without breakfast and had an overall unkempt appearance. They also had not been bringing in their homework. When asked about this, one of them responded, "Shirley didn't make me do it."

The guidance counselor called Shirley's mother to see if anything was wrong. Mrs. Rolph reported that things were better than ever. Mr. Rolph had successfully completed his latest round of rehabilitation and was not drinking. He was home with the family once again after an absence of almost a year and was looking for a job. Mrs. Rolph agreed to allow the school psychologist to speak with Shirley.

During the interview with the school psychologist Shirley said very little. She just sat with her head bowed and said that nothing was wrong. She promised to do better and apologized for neglecting her younger siblings. The psychologist felt that she was being sexually abused, perhaps by Mr. Rolph. However, he had no evidence to back up his hunches.

Questions for reflection and discussion:

1. Without any evidence, what can the psychologist do to act on his suspicions? Should he share his hunches with anyone else, i.e. school personnel, Shirley's mother, Shirley's pediatrician?

2. What signs could Shirley's teachers look for that may point to sexual abuse?

3. Is it possible that the psychologist is mistaken and that Shirley's sudden personality change is due to other factors? What else could be causing her sudden change?

4. Would it have been better if a female psychologist or therapist had talked to Shirley?

5. Should Mr. Rolph be confronted with the psychologist's suspicions? If so, how should it be presented?

6. If the psychologist is unable to substantiate sexual abuse, what actions can the school take to protect Shirley? What actions can be taken to help her deal with whatever has caused her sudden personality change?

Chapter 8

Attention Deficit Hyperactivity Disorder: The Inability to Focus

Mr. Lopez was exhausted. He was teaching the first grade for the first time. He wondered if he had made a mistake by transferring from the fourth grade. He had needed a change and had jumped at the opportunity to work with younger children. But he was totally unprepared for what he faced.

The first graders were much less independent than the fourth graders. They couldn't seem to do anything by themselves. He knew that he would get used to this, but he wasn't sure he'd ever get used to Donna. Donna was a whirlwind. If he wasn't giving her one-on-one instruction, Donna was all over the place. She would get up out of her seat, roam around the room, bother other students, write on the blackboard, and even run up and down the aisles. She just couldn't seem to sit still for a minute. Her attention span seemed to be about 30 seconds.

Mr. Lopez wondered if Donna might not have attention deficit hyperactivity disorder. He had taught students with ADHD before, but by the time they got to the fourth grade they were medicated. Mr. Lopez didn't really know what the symptoms of ADHD were since he had never before been involved in the identification or diagnosis of the disorder.

The guidance counselor had given him a referral form and checklist to fill out, but explained that the diagnostic process would take time. If Donna did have ADHD, and if medication was recommended, it probably would be several weeks or months before this happened. Mr. Lopez didn't know if he would survive. He needed help now.

Attention Deficit Hyperactivity Disorder (ADHD) is a new name for a syndrome that came to the attention of the medical community around 1950 when educators noticed that a number of students could not pay attention, were too easily distracted, could not focus their concentration, could not follow a simple set of instructions, and were overly active. Various opinions exist as to the cause of ADHD. It has been theorized that it is inherited, results from abnormal brain chemistry, is caused by illness or trauma to the brain, or results from delayed development of brain tissue. Regardless, the medical community generally feels that students with ADHD are neurologically different.

In the classroom students with ADHD generally have difficulty focusing their attention on a task for more than a few seconds, are easily distracted, and sometimes are disruptive. These children are challenging to a classroom teacher because they can act without thinking and expect their demands and needs to be met immediately. One or two children with ADHD in a classroom can require as much of the teacher's attention as the other 23 students combined. Physically, these students may be hyperactive, exhibiting little control over bodily movements. Many appear to be in a constant whirlwind; unable to sit still or even remain seated, constantly disrupting the lesson by shouting out, angering their classmates by impulsively lashing out at them, etc. Consequently, they are not adept in social situations.

Students with ADHD are challenging learners as well. Their short attention spans, poor organizational skills, and inability to focus their attention on classroom instruction often result in poor academic achievement. Many have emotional problems resulting from their inability to understand their own behavior, the constant criticism they are subjected to, and their inability to make and maintain positive peer relationships.

ADHD is a medical condition that can be diagnosed only by a qualified physician such as a neurologist. Treatment may involve a medical regimen but often also may include counseling and educational interventions. Most of the classroom strategies that have proven to be successful involve the imposition of external controls on the student. Structure and organization must be provided by others. These students benefit from consistent daily routines, consistent application of classroom rules, and consistent discipline. It is also important for teachers to recognize and make allowances for the student's immaturity, poor organization, and sometimes lowered achievement level. It is also helpful to vary student activities to maintain student interest.

Compassion is probably the most important ingredient to successfully working with a child who has ADHD. It is important to remember that the child is not responsible for the syndrome and cannot control all of his or her actions. The teacher who loses patience or gets frustrated will only make the situation worse.

Additional Reading

Anastopoulos, A., DuPaul, G., and Barkley, R. (1991). Stimulant medication and parent training therapies for attention-deficit hyperactivity disorder. *Journal of Learning Disabilities, 24(4)*, 210–218.

Burcham, B., Carlson, L., and Milich, R. (1993). Promising school-based practices for students with attention deficit disorder. *Exceptional Children, 60*, 174–180.

Council for Exceptional Children. (1992). *Children with ADD: A Shared Responsibility*. Reston, VA: Author.

Forness, S., Swanson, J., Cantwell, D., Guthrie, D. and Sena, R. (1992). Response to stimulant medication across six measures of school-related performance in children with ADHD and disruptive behavior. *Journal of the Council for Children with Behavior Disorders, 18(1)*, 42–53.

Fouse, B., and Brians S. (1993). *A Primer on Attention Deficit Disorder*. Bloomington, IN: Phi Delta Kappa Educational Foundation.

Gadow, K. (1986). *Children on Medication, Volumes I and II*. San Diego, CA: College-Hill Press.

Hallowell, E.M., and Ratey, J.J. (1994). *Driven to Distraction: Recognizing and Coping with Attention Deficit Disorder from Childhood to Adulthood*. New York: Simon & Schuster.

Harvard Medical School. (1985). Attention deficit disorder. *Mental Health Letter, 2(3)*. Cambridge, MA: Author.

Jordan, D.R. (1988). *Attention Deficit Disorder: ADD Syndrome*. Austin, TX: Pro-Ed.

Kneedler, R.D., and Hallahan, D.P. (1981). Self-monitoring of on-task behavior with learning-disabled children: current studies and directions. *Exceptional Education Quarterly, 2(3)*, 73–82.

Macht, J. (1990). *Managing classroom behavior: An Ecological Approach to Academic and Social Learning*. New York: Longman, Inc.

McKinney, J.D., Montague, M., and Hocutt, A.M. (1993). Educational assessment of students with attention deficit disorder. *Exceptional Children, 60*, 125–131.

Silver, L. (1990). Attention deficit-hyperactivity disorder: Is it a learning disability or a related disorder? *Journal of Learning Disabilities 23(7)*, 394–397.

Zentall, S.S. (1993). Research on the educational implications of attention deficit hyperactivity disorder. *Exceptional Children, 60*, 143–153.

Case Studies

Case Study #8-1

Student: Anna

Background: Anna is a nine year old third grade student attending an inner-city school. She lives with her mother (age 26) and two sisters (ages 10 and 6) in subsidized housing. The family has not had contact with Anna's father since her six year old sister was born. Anna's mother has a history of drug abuse but has been clean for three years. Very little is known about Anna's father except that he was physically abusive. Anna's maternal grandmother lives nearby and exerts a great influence over Anna's mother.

Anna was referred for a special education evaluation in kindergarten because of learning problems. An Individualized Education Program (IEP) was developed to address those problems and she attended a transitional first grade classroom the following year. The next year she attended a standard first grade classroom with resource room instruction in reading and language arts. During that year she began to exhibit behavioral problems, was inattentive, and seemed to have difficulty concentrating. At one point, during the administration of standardized group tests in the classroom, Anna stood on her chair and screamed, "I can't do it!"

Anna was evaluated by a neurologist who diagnosed her as having an attention deficit disorder. Stimulant medication was prescribed; however, Anna's mother never filled the prescription because grandmother objected, stating, "She doesn't need drugs to make her behave. A good whipping ought to do it." School officials and the neurologist have spoken to the grandmother in an attempt to educate her about ADHD and stimulant medication. She responded by stating that it was "nothing but a bunch of crap." Although Anna experienced problems in the classroom she was successful in the resource room and did not exhibit behavior problems there.

In grade two Anna had a very good year. Her special education services were increased and she participated in group counseling sessions. Her teacher was very understanding and worked hard to meet Anna's academic and social/emotional needs. Although she still exhibited some behavioral problems, it was felt that she was in control. Her special education teacher felt she made great strides academically and behaviorally that year.

Presenting problem: Anna's third grade experience has not been positive. She was placed in a classroom with a former remedial reading teacher who is in a classroom situation for the first time. This teacher has an excellent reputation as a strict disciplinarian and as an effective teacher. She has high academic and behavioral standards but is somewhat inflexible in the application of those standards.

Anna's behavior problems have escalated. She has defied the authority of her teacher and the principal on numerous occasions and has assaulted other students. She is very impulsive and her teacher claims that she creates a constant disruptive atmosphere in the classroom by shouting out, wandering about the room at will, arguing with classmates and the teacher, refusing to do assignments, leaving the classroom without permission, etc.

When she is disruptive she is removed from the classroom and works in the assistant principal's office with an instructional aide. This occurs on an almost daily basis. Anna has been suspended twice for assaulting other students. Her mother agreed to a trial of Ritalin; however, after one month it does not appear to be of any benefit. In fact, the special education teacher feels that Anna is angrier and has been more aggressive since she started taking medication.

Since Anna's behavior worsens as the day goes on, she has been placed on a reduced day program. She attends school for only three hours a day and is in the resource room for half that time. Her behavior in the resource room is no better than it is in the classroom and her once-positive relationship with the resource room teacher has deteriorated. School personnel are currently considering placement in a self-contained special education class for students with behavioral disorders. Anna's mother has asked if there is a "reform school" that Anna could be sent to.

Anna's mother has also told the guidance counselor that she is concerned that Anna's two sisters are being negatively affected by Anna's problems. The older sister has always been a good student but has suddenly stopped doing her homework. The younger sister was recently diagnosed as having learning disabilities and one day came crying to her mother that she didn't "want to be like Anna."

Questions for reflection and discussion:

1. On a recent occasion when Anna was sent to the assistant principal's office she screamed to her teacher, "All you ever do is send me to the office." Since this "time-out" has not been effective, should it be continued? What other alternatives could Anna's teacher use when her behavior in the classroom is out-of-control?

2. The medication has not had an effect on Anna's classroom behavior. What steps should be taken regarding this situation?

3. The school district is considering a full-time special education class placement. Does this step seem warranted or is it premature? Could other alternatives in a less restrictive setting be tried first?

4. Anna's mother reports that Anna's siblings have been affected by her school difficulties. The older sister, who has always been a good student, has suddenly stopped doing her homework. The younger sister has been diagnosed as having learning disabilities and has expressed the fear that she's going to be like Anna. What support services can be given to the family?

5. The school's principal feels that a personal conflict may have developed between Anna and her teacher. Would a transfer to another classroom be appropriate? Why or why not?

Case Study #8-2

Student: Desmond

Background: Desmond is a 10 year old fourth grader attending a large elementary school. Desmond and his younger half-brother live with a maternal aunt, uncle, and three cousins. Desmond's mother is a drug addict who has been in and out of rehabilitation facilities for several years. She was actively using drugs when Desmond was born. His father was killed during an altercation in a bar three years ago. As Desmond puts it, "He got in a fight with some guy and the guy got a gun and blew him away." Desmond has responded well to the structure, discipline, and nurturing of his aunt's home, but says that he wished he could live with his mother. At the present time his aunt is attempting to gain permanent custody because Desmond's mother's drug rehabilitation is not succeeding. Desmond realizes that his mother is "sick" and that it is unlikely that she will get better.

Desmond has suffered several disappointments on his way to realizing that he may never again live with his mother. She has not shown up for numerous scheduled visits. When she does visit she is often under the influence of drugs so that Desmond's aunt will not allow her to take the children out of the house. On one occasion the police had to remove her from the house because she refused to leave without the children. His mother was unable to make Desmond's first communion and his karate class award ceremony, although she had promised to be present for both. Desmond reacted to these disappointments by taking out his anger on significant adults: his aunt, uncle, and teachers.

Desmond receives resource room services for reading and math. He is approximately two years below grade level expectations in each of these subjects in spite of average intelligence and no evidence of learning disabilities. He is receiving counseling at a local mental health clinic.

Presenting problem: Desmond's classroom teacher has asked the pupil personnel services team for help in dealing with his classroom behavior. She reports that he is not a bad kid but is constantly disrupting the classroom. Much of Desmond's behavior can be characterized as attention-seeking. For example, if the class is having a discussion, Desmond will add a gross tidbit to the conversation. In a recent discussion about animals, Desmond related a story about the family cat getting run over by his mother's boyfriend. Desmond proceeded to describe in graphic detail how the late cat looked following its premature demise. Desmond seemed to enjoy the looks of disgust on the faces of his classmates.

His teacher reports that Desmond is constantly out of his seat bothering other students, pokes other students with his pencil or ruler, blurts out answers and comments without raising his hand, and frequently interrupts lessons with comments that have no relevance to the topic at hand. He is more concerned with what other students are doing than he is with himself. Desmond constantly complains that other students are bothering him; but, when the complaint is investigated it turns out that he was the instigator.

Desmond's peer relations are poor. Other students do not want to sit near him or work with him in a group. They complain that he makes comments with sexual innuendos. Desmond denies making these comments. When he is caught misbehaving, he always blames his problems on another student, i.e. "Danny was talking to me and I was telling him to be quiet." Desmond's teacher uses cooperative learning strategies in her classroom but reports that they do not work with Desmond as other students object to having him in their groups.

Academically, Desmond is not passing the fourth grade. His teacher has recommended retention but the principal is not sure this a good idea. Most written assignments are not completed or are completed with little concern for quality. He does not proofread his work or check the accuracy of his answers. Homework is passed in approximately 25% of the time. Desmond's aunt insists that he does his homework, but he can never find it when it's time to pass it in. In spite of his low grades and risk of not passing, Desmond's teacher reports that his behavior is a greater concern.

Desmond's teacher has raised the question of whether he has an attention deficit disorder. The special education teacher reports that Desmond has many of the symptoms of ADD/ADHD: He is highly distractable, has a very short attention span, is impulsive, etc. However, Desmond's counselor and pediatrician feel that his attentional problems are caused by emotional concerns rather than ADD/ADHD. Before Desmond came to live with his aunt, the school psychologist in his previous school system recommended a neurological evaluation; however, he has never been evaluated by a neurologist. The special education teacher has found that prefocusing activities and constant monitoring are sufficient to keep Desmond on task. The classroom teacher has employed these tactics, but with 22 other students has found that they are not as effective in the classroom as they are in the resource room. She is looking for a management system that will work in the general education setting.

Questions for reflection and discussion:

1. Prior to coming to live with his aunt, the school psychologist in Desmond's previous school recommended a neurological evaluation. This evaluation was never completed. The pupil personnel services team at his current school have deferred to the judgment of his counselor and pediatrician and have not pursued a neurological evaluation. Should a neurological

evaluation be conducted to rule out a biological basis for Desmond's behavior?

2. How much of Desmond's behavior is related to his mother's behavior? Could the current custody proceedings be contributing to his behavior?

3. What type of classroom management system would best address Desmond's needs and his teacher's needs?

4. Desmond's aunt and uncle report that they are having similar problems with him at home regarding his relations with his cousins and neighborhood children. Could a home component of his behavior management system be developed?

5. The principal is skeptical about retaining Desmond in grade four. Is retention a good idea? What other alternatives could be pursued?

Case Study #8-3

Student: Nathan

Background: Nathan is a five year old kindergarten student who has had no prior educational experiences. His parents are divorced and his father has remarried. The parents separated shortly after Nathan's birth. Nathan lives with his mother and older brother. He visits his father every weekend. His mother has a history of substance abuse problems. Nathan's older brother, James, who is now in the third grade, was diagnosed as having ADD/ADHD when he was in the first grade. Medication was prescribed but was discontinued earlier this year after his mother started taking it. The state Department of Social Services is involved with the family and the mother is undergoing treatment for her addiction. Nathan is attending a public school kindergarten class. There are 23 students in the class. His teacher is very experienced, having taught kindergarten for nine years.

Presenting Problem: Nathan is having a difficult time in kindergarten. He flits from activity to activity but never seems to find one that can hold his interest. He finds it nearly impossible to sit at his seat for longer than a few minutes. He often has to be removed from the group when the teacher reads to the class because he is unable to sit still and listen. His excessive movements disturb the other children.

Nathan is a charming five year old. He has a quick smile and eyes that literally light up when he is amused. He is affectionate and enjoys being hugged. However, he is not very popular among his classmates. Nathan is impulsive and frequently grabs toys and other materials from other students. When spoken to about this behavior, Nathan is always sorry; but the behavior continues. If another student takes something from Nathan, he reacts by hitting or kicking the other student. He does not willingly share with other students. Recently, Nathan took a handful of finger paint and smeared it on a young girl's hair. When spoken to about the incident the only reason he could offer for his behavior was that he was mad because her picture was better than his.

A comprehensive special education evaluation revealed that Nathan has average intellectual potential. Deficits were noted on subtests that required immediate concentration, attention to task, and short-term memory. Conversely, tasks requiring long-term memory were a strength. In spite of having average potential, Nathan's teacher reported that he was not making progress and she feels that he is not ready for first grade.

Nathan's mother reports that she does not have too many problems with him at home, although he fights with his brother frequently. She indicated that he does not watch much television, preferring to play outside. He likes to make up games where he is a monster chasing other children. She agrees that even at home he does not stick to one activity for very long. Both boys enjoy their weekends with their father because they get to do "neat stuff." Their father is an outdoorsman who takes them camping and engages them in many outdoor activities.

A neurological evaluation was recommended but was not pursued because the neurologist that had treated James informed his mother that he would not prescribe medication for a child under the age of six. School personnel have decided not to push the issue at this time because of the incident with the mother taking James' medication.

Questions for Reflection and Discussion:

1. Nathan's teacher feels that he is not ready for first grade. The school has three options available: a) retention in kindergarten, b) placement in a transitional first grade, or c) placement in a special education classroom. Which of the three options would be best? Why?
2. Medication does not appear to be an option at the present time. What specific strategies could be employed to increase Nathan's attention span and decrease his impulsivity?
3. The family is currently involved with the Department of Social Services. Part of that program includes family counseling around issues of mother's substance abuse and the boys' frequent fighting. Would school-based counseling also be advisable?
4. Although Nathan's mother does not view his behavior at home as a problem, would a behavior management system with a home component be feasible? If so, what kinds of follow-up in the home would be needed?
5. Nathan has never had a neurological evaluation. Should he have one even though the neurologist will not prescribe medication? Is it feasible to consider medication sometime in the future?

Case Study #8-4

Student: Justin

Background: Justin is a 13 year old eighth grader who was diagnosed as having an attention deficit disorder in first grade. He has taken stimulant medication since that time. Justin lives with his mother. Until recently a step-father and two step-sisters also lived with them. Justin's mother and step-father have separated although there is a possibility of a reconciliation. Justin was not particularly close to his step-father, but was close to his youngest step-sister. His mother works as an aerobics instructor at a health club. His father lives in a distant state and Justin has not visited him for several years. The last time he did visit problems developed between Justin and his father's new wife. Justin is a bright student who has never experienced any academic problems. He has never received special education services. For several years he received counseling at a local mental health clinic. He has never been labeled a discipline problem, although he has occasionally been sent to the office because of classroom disruptions. This usually occurred when he had forgotten to take his medication in the morning.

Presenting Problem: Shortly after his mother and step-father separated Justin refused to take his medication. Initially, he claimed his refusal was due to the fact that he didn't want to be treated differently. However, he has also expressed the opinion that his medication is a drug and he doesn't want to be a druggie. The school counselor has tried to talk to him about this, but Justin is adamant that he is not going to take the medication. His physician switched him to a time-release medication so that he doesn't have to take it during school hours; however, this has not made a difference in Justin's attitude.

Unfortunately since Justin has stopped taking the medication his grades and overall behavior have worsened. His teachers describe him as being the class clown. He makes noises and comments in class that his classmates find amusing but his teachers do not. He once arrived on the gymnasium floor wearing his athletic supporter over his gym shorts and his sneakers on the wrong feet. He has been given numerous detentions and received a one day in-building suspension but has not received any other disciplinary sanctions.

Justin rarely completes an assignment and generally forgets his homework. His teachers also report that he does not come to class prepared and with the proper materials. He is extremely disorganized. Failing grades on his last report card have not given him the incentive to begin his medication again. At this point Justin is in danger of repeating the eighth grade. At a recent parent-teacher conference, Justin's mother could offer no explanation for his behavior or poor attitude. She said she would try to get his step-father to talk to him. She indicated a willingness to look into counseling again but fears that Justin may not cooperate.

Questions for Reflection and Discussion:

1. Justin's mother is willing to consider counseling again but fears that he will not go. What incentives could be provided so that Justin will attend counseling sessions and be cooperative?
2. Although medication seemed to solve Justin's ADD/ADHD problems the reality of the situation is that Justin is not currently taking it. What strategies can his teachers employ to improve his overall behavior and academic performance?
3. What effect could Justin's mother's separation from his step-father have on his current attitude? Remember, Justin was not particularly close to his step-father but was close to his youngest step-sister.
4. Justin has not seen his father for several years although he does have contact with him. Would a visit to his father be helpful?
5. Justin's neurologist has suggested that a complete physical may be in order. How could this provide insight into Justin's current attitude?

Case Study #8-5

Student: Donny

Background: Donny is a 16 year old sophomore attending a comprehensive high school. He lives with his mother, her boyfriend, and a six month old sister. Donny's father lives in another state and he has not seen him for years. Donny's maternal grandparents are very involved in his life and have taken much of the responsibility for his upbringing. Donny's mother appears to be very limited intellectually; however, Mrs. T.'s mother reported to a counselor that she was once an excellent student who "literally fried her brain on drugs." Apparently she was an active user when Donny was conceived.

Donny underwent a full special education evaluation in the second grade after being referred because he was unable to complete any assignments and cried often in class. The evaluation indicated that he has an I.Q. in the superior range. Although the evaluation team found that he did not have any special education needs, it did recommend a complete neurological evaluation. As a result of the neurological evaluation stimulant medication was prescribed but his mother did not fill the prescription. At a conference Donny's mother indicated that she did not get the prescription filled because her mother was opposed to "putting him on medication to make him behave." She did, however, agree to take him for counseling.

After many attempts to persuade Donny's mother to agree to a trial of medication failed, school officials held a conference that included Donny's grandparents. After the situation was explained thoroughly, Donny's grand-mother finally consented to a one-month trial of medication. The change in Donny's ability to complete assignments and in the overall quality of his work was so remarkable that his teachers commented that he should be the "poster boy for the ADHD association." From that point on Donny was very successful academically and even made high honors throughout middle school. Upon entering high school he was placed in a college-preparatory program. He finished ninth grade with a 95 average. Unfortunately, since he was doing well in school, his mother withdrew him from counseling.

Presenting problem: Several weeks into his sophomore year Donny suddenly stopped taking his medication. His grades dropped drastically and he became a behavior problem in class. His teachers described his behaviors as being of the nuisance-type: talking in class, disturbing other students, arriving late, coming unprepared, etc. He was failing four out of five major subjects at the end of the first marking period. He was referred to the guidance counselor when a teacher monitoring an after school detention overheard him say that life sucked and he'd like to end it all. During a discussion with the guidance counselor the next day, Donny assured her that he would not kill himself. He informed the counselor that the reason he was not taking his medication was that the prescription had expired and his mother refused to take him to the doctor to get it refilled. According to Donny his mother said that he shouldn't need that stuff at his age. He also stated that his mother really didn't care about him since the baby was born.

The counselor called Donny's mother in for a conference. Mrs. T. insisted that Donny's story about her not refilling his medication was not true. She stated that they had plenty of pills but that Donny refused to take them. She said that he had become very rebellious since the baby was born and she thought he was jealous. She also said that Donny resented her boyfriend because of his different ethnic background. In addition it was learned that Donny's grandparents had separated after nearly 40 years of marriage.

Donny's grades continued their downward spiral and he appeared to become more depressed as time went on. His teachers and counselors suspected that he was using drugs. He appeared to be stoned many mornings and began to neglect his personal hygiene. He was also hanging out with other suspected drug users.

Questions for Reflection and Discussion:

1. How can school officials find out who is telling the truth — Donny or his mother?

2. How may the changes in Donny's personal life (i.e. new baby, presence of mother's boyfriend, grandparents' separation) have affected his ability to control his own ADHD?

3. Teachers are afraid that Donny may be "self-medicating" by using illegal drugs. Is this a possibility? What steps should be taken to find out and deal with this problem if it is true?

4. Does the fact that Donny's mother withdrew him from counseling in elementary school have any bearing on his later difficulties in high school after so many years of success? Is it too late for counseling now?

5. What steps should school officials take to get Donny back on a track of academic success again?

6. Is Donny a high risk for dropping out of school? If he is, what can be done to intervene?

Chapter 9

Attention Seeking Behaviors: The Need to Belong

George Vernon, the Dean of Students at Central High School, had just returned from the emergency room of General Hospital. One of Central's sophomore students, Lisa, had been taken there by ambulance because she had fallen down a flight of stairs and broken a leg. It was the third time this year that Lisa had broken a bone. In the fall she had broken a wrist playing field hockey and a few months ago she broke a collar bone doing a vault in gymnastics.

Lisa was known to be quite an actress. She can become very melodramatic at the slightest injury. She spent so much time in the nurse's office in the past that the nurse threatened to charge her rent. Everyone had felt that most of Lisa's past injuries were a figment of her imagination and a means of drawing attention to herself. She seemed to enjoy wearing an elastic bandage and having others ask her what had happened.

The staff had decided to try to ignore Lisa's injuries and complaints. That's when the broken bones started. George wondered, "Would Lisa go so far as to throw herself down the stairs to get attention?" It sounded far-fetched, but he wouldn't put it past her. Perhaps they had made a mistake by ignoring her minor injuries.

In this chapter selected issues involved in responding to attention seeking behaviors of students in classroom settings will be discussed. Such behaviors are especially irritating and interfere with classroom routines. They result in disrupting the flow and pace of classroom lessons and serve to decrease student focus on tasks. Such behavior is not generally considered a severe indication of a lack of internal adaptive controls, and can often be exhibited by more than a single student at the same time. Due to this latter reason, attention seeking behaviors can cause major difficulties for teachers and other students in the classroom. When they interfere directly with the learning space to which all students are entitled, teacher action is necessary to both correct and prevent continual occurrence.

What are some characteristics of attention seeking behaviors? The most noticeable of these are those behaviors that draw adult attention such as calling out, getting up from one's desk and wandering around the classroom, frequent need to retrieve materials, pencils in need of sharpening, over-dependence on teacher time for explanations and help, making noises and use of body language to get the attention of peers, etc. The purpose of attention seeking behaviors can be to draw attention from adults as well as from peers. However, their greater purpose is to acquire the exclusive attention of the teacher.

What might be some intrinsic motivational causes of such attention seeking? Experts often suggest that what might explain such behavior is the fact that the student simply is unwilling to share any part of the attending adult with anyone else and must learn new behaviors that allow for such experience. Others might suggest that such behaviors in the past have allowed a child to get what he/she wants; in other words, the child will use the behavior that has worked in the past. Again, there is a need for the child to learn new ways of communicating. Still others will suggest that the student who uses behavior as an attention device is discouraged in his/her own ability to succeed in school like other children. The causal factor in this view is the motivation to belong as a member of the class. It should be pointed out that such behaviors in classrooms have as their purpose drawing attention from others, regardless of whether the attention is positive or negative. Most often it is the latter.

What makes such behavior so troubling is that with an increase of diverse learners in regular classroom settings there is a greater chance that the need for each student to take his/her rightful place as a class member can be jeopardized. This may result from the inability of the teacher to respond effectively to a natural increase in the incidence of attention seeking symptoms among such diverse student classroom groups. Until those who control the distribution of resource allocations recognize the influence on learning that diverse developmental needs of students present, the need for teacher assistance in regular classroom settings will continue to go unanswered.

The basic need to belong, to be connected, and to be part of the class of children has received attention elsewhere in this text as well. Glasser identifies such connectedness as one of four basic needs of all individuals.[1] Maslow in his seminal work on becoming a person writes about the motivational forces that drive all human behavior from a hierarchy of human needs.[2] Most basic among them are the physiological and psychological needs to feel secure as a person. Thus the need to belong has long been recognized as being a powerful stimulus for expression of what an individual perceives as his/her needs.

The idea that attention seeking behavior in the classroom can reflect a student's self-perception of personal discouragement may be more accu-

1. Glasser, W. (1965). *Reality Therapy: A New Approach to Psychiatry.* New York: Harper Calophon Books.
2. Maslow, A. (1962). *Toward a Psychology of Being.* Princeton: Van Nostrand.

rate than previously thought. What then, are some implications for teachers in the classroom setting experiencing such attention seeking behaviors from their students? Again we are reminded of the importance of the internal dialogue as a first step in the problem solving process, to produce a consciousness-raising effect. The major implication for the teacher is to meet the attention seeker's need for recognition while not taking away from others. In the long term the attention seeker must be weaned from this behavior and learn to accept other more positive means of internal gratification.

Additional Reading

Glasser, W. (1965). *Reality Therapy: A New Approach to Psychiatry.* New York: Harper Calophon Books.

Glasser, W. (1992). *The Quality School: Managing Students Without Coercion* (2nd Ed.). New York: Harper-Collins.

Glasser, W. (1993). *The Quality School Teacher*. New York: Harper-Collins.

Kuhns, C.L., and Marcus, R. (1992). Maternal child-rearing practices and children's social problem solving skills. *ERIC Document Reproduction Service* ED352571.

Mace, F.C. et al. (1991). Functional analysis and treatment of aberrant behavior. *Research in Developmental Disabilities, 12(2)*, 155–189.

McNamee-McGrory, V., and Cipani, E. (1995). Reduction of inappropriate "clinging" behaviors in a preschooler through social skills training and utilization of the "Premack" principle. *ERIC Document Reproduction Service* ED401001.

Murphy, L. and Della Corte, S. (1990). School-related stress and the special child. *ERIC Document Reproduction Service* ED318178.

Shaw, D.S. et al. (1994). Developmental precursors of externalizing behavior: Ages 1 to 3. *Developmental Psychology, 30(3)*, 355–364.

Taylor, J.C. (1994). Functional assessment and functionally-derived treatment for child behavior problems. *Special Services in the Schools, 9(1)*, 39–67.

Williams, C. et al. (1990). Ratings of behavior problems in adolescents hospitalized for substance abuse. *Journal of Adolescent Chemical Dependency, 1(1)*, 95–112.

Case Studies

Case Study #9-1

Student: Melissa

Background: Melissa is a small, attractively dressed, 10 year old racially-mixed child who wears her hair in pigtails and carries a small doll wherever she goes. She seems withdrawn and shy, rarely initiates speech, and often will only respond to conversation with nods and other gestures. She is the sixth child of a white mother who relies on welfare for the family's support and whose children all have different black fathers. The older children have multiple serious psycho-social problems that include hard drug usage, anti-social gang related behavior, sexual overtness, multiple illegitimacies, and have served prison time for such crimes as rape, attempted murder of a police officer, and drug dealing. All have racial identify confusion.

Melissa had been seen for several years by community mental health professionals who have observed her growth in spite of the turbulent origins and family problems. She exhibits real confusion and disorientation at times, and occasionally seems out of contact with reality. Since she uses similar behavior as an avoidance tactic, it is difficult to know when she is really disordered and when she is manipulating. Also, she is a clever and persistent thief. What is fascinating, however, is that academically Melissa performs close to her grade level which is estimated as grade five. However, there is little evidence of any formal schooling which is attributed to the numerous family moves. Attempts to piece together a complete set of school records have not been successful. Melissa's basic reading, math, spelling, social studies, and science skills appear to be within the normal range. She does, however, avoid arts and crafts activities, claiming they are a waste of time.

While Melissa's performance appears to be age appropriate, she is not consistent in her classroom work, falling behind, and routinely failing except when she has received special exclusive adult attention. It is obvious that Melissa is invested in failure because it is failure that will bring her the special attention with an adult for the support and encouragement she direly needs. She seems to control resistance as a manipulative tool and is very strong in her attempts to demand exclusive adult attention. Melissa does seem to prefer attention from females and shuns male overtures. Recently, she shocked a male counselor who came to see her for assessment purposes. She asked aloud in response to his request for her to accompany him to his office, "Are you going to molest me?" The counselor, being relatively young and inexperienced, was so taken aback that he lost all composure.

Presenting problem: Melissa was enrolled as a diagnostic student in Mrs. Wallace's resource room for the past four weeks. When she was verbally teased by another student named Ronnie, she responded very violently by stabbing him in the eye with a sharp pencil, inflicting a rather serious wound. Other past aggressive behavioral reactions have included clawing, slapping, and hitting, which she often displays even without being provoked. When she is unable to receive individual attention from someone or from a group of individuals, Melissa laughs out loud at their mistakes or surreptitiously gives them the finger. She has seemingly destroyed all possibilities of establishing positive relations with her peers.

On the other hand, Melissa can also be highly manipulative by using a "poor little frightened child" mannerism to attract the interest and concern of adults. She utilizes this pathetic behavioral response to exclude all other children from the present adult's attention and secures a constant one-to-one relationship with that person. If this form of manipulation fails, she resorts to isolating the adult with persistent aggression toward other children or through other disruptive behaviors that evidences genuine gratification at the negative attention she receives.

Melissa was placed in the resource room because of her behavior problems as identified by the county mental health office. Mrs. Wallace has a superb reputation for her ability to work with all kinds of children and is known to view students such as Melissa as challenges rather than as problems. However, Melissa's behavior is now out of control, even for her excellent teacher. Mrs. Wallace's primary task is to collect assessment data on classroom functioning levels using criterion referenced instruments so that the school's evaluation team can make an appropriate determination as to what Melissa's exact needs are.

Questions for reflection and discussion:

1. What are the reasons for Melissa's need for adult attention, even negative attention? Why is this expressed in the form of rage?
2. In the short period of time Mrs. Wallace may have with her, what strategies can she implement to channel Melissa's behavior in a more positive direction? What can be done to repair Melissa's peer relationships? How can Mrs. Wallace protect the other students from Melissa?
3. What types of assessment data should Mrs. Wallace gather to help develop an appropriate placement and program for Melissa? What type of placement would be best for Melissa?
4. When Melissa is placed in a permanent program, what types of support services will she require? What types of family services would be helpful?
5. What is the long-term prognosis for a child such as Melissa?

Case Study #9-2

Student: Raphael

Background: Raphael is a sixth grade student who has been placed in a full time special education class due to a diagnosis of behaviorally disordered. He is mainstreamed for two periods a day. However, if he is unable to cooperate in the mainstream classroom he is returned to the special education class and is given time out. The time out area consists of a study carrel where his teacher, Mr. Henry, can observe him. While in time out he is not allowed any interaction with either his peers or adults and is not provided with any learning materials. He must sit quietly for five minutes before he is allowed to leave the time out area.

There are seven other students in the classroom. In addition to Mr. Henry, the class has a student teacher, Ms. Carol, from the local university, and a paraprofessional. Ms. Carol is working on a master's degree with a specialization in teaching the emotionally disturbed and behaviorally disordered. The paraprofessional's primary responsibility is to accompany the students to their mainstream classrooms and assist the teacher there. The students in the special education class have a number of things in common: they come from dysfunctional homes, generally the father is absent, a family history of alcohol and/or drug abuse, court or Department of Social Services involvement. The special education classroom is probably the only place where the children receive consistent support and structure to help them grow and develop. The mainstream classroom teachers are aware that these children have emotional and behavioral problems but are not privy to their family histories and backgrounds.

Raphael's mother is a recovering alcoholic and his father is in jail. Raphael once wrote a letter to his father in jail. His father replied inquiring as to how old he was and what grade he was in. His mother is very strict and sets rigid rules that even the Department of Social Services' social worker feels are unreasonable. However, the social worker is unable to convince his mother to deal with him in any other manner. His mother comes down hard on him for even minor infractions and generally conveys an attitude that Raphael cannot do anything right. She makes numerous promises to him but rarely keeps them. There is little consistency and predictability in the home. Due to these home circumstances Raphael does not respond well to adults in authority. When disciplined, he is very defensive and his teachers have great difficulty getting him to understand what he has done wrong. His perception of the incident is usually quite different from that of others, even adults who have witnessed it. Disciplinary situations usually end up with Raphael feeling that once again, the adults in control are out to get him.

Presenting problem: This morning, while working in a small group activity with four other students in one of his mainstream classes, Raphael took a small model car out of his pocket and began playing with it. Noting that he was off-task, the teacher reminded him several times that he needed to focus his attention on the task at hand. When he ignored these overtures she reminded him that he needed to pay attention, follow instructions, and stay on-task to be successful in her classroom. Instead of responding by getting back to work, Raphael began to mimic the teacher. She warned him that if he wasn't respectful he would have to go back to his special education class. Raphael belligerently responded by saying that he wasn't doing anything wrong and continued with his disrespectful behavior. When the teacher tried to explain how his behavior was inappropriate, Raphael told her that she was just like everyone else, always trying to boss him around. He ended by telling her to go #$%& herself. Raphael was immediately returned to his special education classroom and was assigned to the time out area.

Both Mr. Henry and Ms. Carol felt disappointed and rejected. They had been working hard with Raphael on his self-control and had felt that he was making very good progress. This incident was definitely a setback. They understood that when Raphael became frustrated he lost his sense of reality and there was no way to reason with him. However, they couldn't understand what caused him to become frustrated in the first place.

Questions for reflection and discussion:

1. What can be done to correct Raphael's perceptions of his teachers? How can he be made to understand that they are not out to get him every time they correct his behavior?

2. How can Raphael be approached so that he doesn't feel so threatened by the adults in the school environment?

3. How can his teachers make Raphael understand that his behavior is often inappropriate and offensive to others?

4. What are Raphael's primary problems? What are the secondary or contributing problems?

5. Should Raphael continue to be mainstreamed? What other supplementary aids and services would help to make the mainstreaming more successful? Should his mainstream teachers be given more information about his family history and background?

6. What is the long term prognosis for Raphael?

Case Study #9-3

Student: Shahab

Background: Shahab is a nine year old third grader who is enrolled in a regular education classroom. He has been in the United States for five months having migrated with his family from Iraq. His family has suffered much hardship and persecution since the Gulf War. Shahab shows little interest in school and his teacher has much difficulty motivating him to complete assignments. There are several other students in his class and school who have come from other countries such as China, Viet Nam, Russia, Cambodia, and Somalia. Most are refugees from some sort of oppression. Shahab receives English as a second language instruction for one hour per day with another student in his class, Daniel.

A student teacher, Miss Kowalski, has been assigned to Shahab's classroom. For the first few weeks of her assignment she spent her time observing, assisting the teacher, and working with small groups of students. After those initial few weeks she took a more active role in the classroom. Miss Kowalski does not agree with the classroom teacher's assessment of Shahab and his situation. During her orientation to the class, the teacher, Mrs. Wilson, informed her that it didn't matter how you treated these foreign students because they wouldn't learn anyway. She also stated that she didn't go along with all this self-esteem business that the experts at the colleges were promoting. Miss Kowalski was surprised at these attitudes. Mrs. Wilson was an experienced, but fairly young teacher, who had attended the same college and even had the same advisor as Miss Kowalski.

Mrs. Wilson seemed overly concerned about the state tests that would be administered in the spring. She preferred to concentrate her efforts on the more able students and practically ignored the ESL students who would be exempted from taking the tests. She stated that she wasn't going to squander the future of her more able students by wasting her time on kids who weren't going to learn anyway. Almost as if to justify her thinking, she stated that she knew the parents of the "American" kids felt the same way.

Miss Kowalski spent as much time as possible working on reading skills with Shahab and the other ESL students in the class. Although they did not read with understanding, they were showing improvement in word recognition skills. She found that they were eager to read and, in fact, seemed to delight in the fact that they were learning English words. It seemed that the more attention she gave them, the more attention they craved. Miss Kowalski was surprised at how well they had progressed. When she told Mrs. Wilson how well they were doing Mrs. Wilson reminded her that she was only a student teacher and did not have the requisite experience to accurately assess their progress. Mrs. Wilson told her that although she meant well she should not be overly optimistic about what these students could accomplish. She ended the conversation by saying, "These kids don't belong in my class so don't get the idea that I should be challenging them more."

After their conversation Miss Kowalski noticed that Mrs. Wilson involved the ESL students in classroom activities even less than before. One day when Mrs. Wilson passed out some papers she did not give any to Shahab and Daniel. When Miss Kowalski brought this oversight to her attention, Mrs. Wilson curtly replied, "They can't do this work." Miss Kowalski politely tried to explain that they could do the assignment if the lesson were modified and they were given some encouragement. Mrs. Wilson did not respond but it was obvious that she was not pleased.

Presenting problem: For the rest of the semester Miss Kowalski tried to give Shahab and the other ESL students as much attention as possible. However, Mrs. Wilson did her best to give her other assignments so that she could not give them as much attention as she would have liked. There was obvious tension between Miss Kowalski and Mrs. Wilson. Since Miss Kowalski recognized that her student teaching grade would depend on Mrs. Wilson's evaluation, she decided that it was best to keep quiet. After all she would never get a teaching job if she didn't get a good grade for her practicum.

As the attention Miss Kowalski paid him diminished, Shahab began to act up in class. He did not present any major problems, rather most of his actions could best be described as attention-seeking. For example, if Miss Kowalski were teaching a lesson to the entire class, Shahab might make funny noises to try to get her attention. Noting this change in behavior, Mrs. Wilson told Miss Kowalski that it was her fault for spoiling the child with "all that extra attention you gave him." Mrs. Wilson responded to Shahab's misbehavior by sending him out into the hallway.

On Miss Kowalski's last day in the classroom, Shahab was unusually quiet. Miss Kowalski tried to talk to him but he just walked away. She sensed that he felt rejected. She told him that although she wouldn't be in the class every day that she would drop in now and then to read with him. Shahab just walked away. As the end of the day was approaching, Miss Kowalski picked out a book and asked Shahab to read it with her. Shahab took the book, threw it across the room, and began to sob. Mrs. Wilson called for the principal to remove him from the classroom. She then turned to Miss Kowalski and said, "See, that's the thanks you get."

Miss Kowalski was shaken by the incident. She decided to immediately drive to the college to see if she could meet with her advisor. As she drove she began to reflect on her entire experience. As she saw it Shahab and Daniel showed little interest in classroom activities because nothing was done to involve them or make them feel like part of the class. They were not motivated because little was expected of them and their accomplishments were not recognized. She felt that something had to be done about how Mrs. Wilson was treating these students. She didn't know what to do but she was no longer willing to remain quiet. She was willing to risk her teaching career for these students.

Questions for reflection and discussion:

1. Why would a young teacher develop the negative attitudes Mrs. Wilson displayed? Could Miss Kowalski have done anything to change those attitudes? Should she have spoken up earlier?
2. What could have been done to engage Shahab, Daniel, and the other ESL students in more class activities? How could they have been better motivated?
3. What does this case study say about teacher expectations?
4. Why did Shahab crave attention when Miss Kowalski was assigned duties that took her away from him? Was Mrs. Wilson right that he had been spoiled by the attention he had been given? If he was, is there anything wrong with being "spoiled" by positive attention?
5. Why did Shahab respond as he did on Miss Kowalski's last day.
6. Is Miss Kowalski's assessment of the classroom situation correct? Why or why not? What can she do about it?

Case Study #9-4

Student: Donna

Background: Donna is a seventh grader who lives with her grandmother and her twin brother Donald. Her father is deceased, having been killed in an automobile accident before her birth. Her mother has remarried and has two other children with her second husband. She lives in a nearby community and Donna and her brother spend weekends with her. Donna and Donald went to live with their grandparents shortly after their birth as their mother was unable to care for them after her first husband's death. Donna's grandfather passed away several years ago. Now that their mother has remarried, it is unclear why the children are not living with her.

Donna's group test scores indicate that her overall achievement levels are below grade level even though she has average intelligence. Two years ago her fifth grade teacher referred her for a special education evaluation because of her underachievement. That evaluation revealed that she was not learning disabled. No reason for her underachievement was ever discovered; however, based on projective tests, the school psychologist suggested that she might have feelings of inadequacy.

Donna's peer relationships are a problem. She is only able to have one friend at a time and that friend may not have any other friends. Donna seems to be totally incapable of being part of a threesome. The problem is that her best friend this week can be her worst enemy next week. This creates serious problems in the classroom as Donna always appears to be the cause of major arguments among the girls in the class, even though she is not directly involved in those arguments. Most of these arguments are over petty issues. The guidance counselor has been able to trace several arguments back to comments (often untrue) Donna has made to one girl about another girl. Donna also doesn't seem to be able to maintain a relationship with any girl for more than a few weeks.

A conference was held several weeks ago with Donna's grandmother to discuss the problem. After the guidance counselor explained the problems Donna was having and recommended counseling, her grandmother suggested that Donna's mother should be part of the discussion. A week later another meeting was held with Donna's mother and step-father. This meeting did not turn out to be very productive, however. Donna's step-father insisted that the problem was not Donna's fault and that the other girls were as much to blame as she was. He demanded that a meeting be set up among the parents of all of the girls involved so that he could confront them concerning their children's harassment of his daughter. The guidance counselor told him that such a meeting was not a good idea but agreed to speak to the parents of the other girls to inform them of the problems the girls were having.

Presenting problem: One day Donna came to the guidance counselor very upset. She dramatically stated that one of the boys, Joshua, was going around telling everyone that he wanted to have sex with her. The guidance counselor told Donna that she would take care of the problem. The counselor immediately went to the vice principal's office where she found Joshua, also very upset. Joshua claimed that Donna was going around telling everyone that he wanted to have sex with her. He insisted that he never said anything of the sort to her or anyone else.

Donna was called back down to the office. The vice principal asked her specifically which students had told her that Joshua said he wanted to have sex with her. Donna gave him several names and he called each of them down. Each student said that he or she had not heard Joshua make any such comments, but that Donna had told them that Joshua wanted to have sex with her. After additional investigation the vice principal determined that Joshua had not said anything but that Donna had been the one spreading the rumor. Donna was called back down to the office and was given a stern warning that she was not to say another word about Joshua wanting to have sex with her. Donna's grandmother was informed of the incident.

At lunch time Donald and Joshua were in a fistfight apparently because Donald felt the need to defend his sister's honor. Witnesses indicated that Donald started the fight by jumping Joshua from behind. Upon questioning Donald, the vice principal found out that Donna had told him that Joshua was spreading lies about her and was telling everyone that he wanted to have sex with her. The vice principal determined that Donna had said this to her brother after he had told her not to say another word about it.

Questions for reflection and discussion:

1. What could be the cause of Donna's peer relationship problem? Is Donna's peer relationship problem connected to her poor academic achievement?

2. Was the school psychologist correct in her diagnosis that Donna has feelings of inadequacy? Is her current behavior connected to those feelings of inadequacy? How?

3. Did the guidance counselor do the right thing by refusing to allow Donna's step-father to confront the parents of the other girls? What else could the counselor have done at this point to deal with Donna's problems?

4. How should the vice principal handle the situation at this point? If Donald is suspended for fighting, should Donna also be suspended? Why or why not?

5. Is this purely a disciplinary matter or is it a problem that needs further intervention? What interventions might be appropriate?

6. Problems such as this can spill over into the classroom. How can the guidance counselor and vice principal work with classroom teachers to prevent this problem from interfering with the classroom routine?

Case Study #9-5

Student: Jimmy

Background: Jimmy is a 10 year old fifth grader who attends the Parkinson Elementary School which is located in a suburban community that has a rich diversity of socioeconomic, cultural, and linguistic groups. The Parkinson School is located in a low income section of the community.

Jimmy is the oldest of four children living with his mother who works as a nurse at the local hospital. She sometimes works weekend shifts and relies on Jimmy to care for his younger siblings. Jimmy's father left the family six years ago. He had a drinking and gambling problem and was abusive toward both mother and children. Jimmy's mother currently has a restraining order against him so that Jimmy has no contact with him at all. His mother is very resentful of the abuse she suffered at his hands. Her resentment extends to members of his family and she has denied visitations with Jimmy's paternal grandparents. She has taken the position that the children can establish contact with their grandparents when they turn 18. A local clergyman, however, is trying to convince her to allow a visitation through the church at a neutral site. Jimmy is excited by this prospect and has been trying particularly hard to behave in hopes that this meeting will materialize.

There are 22 students in Jimmy's classroom. Many of them present significant behavioral challenges to their teacher, Mrs. Winston. Mrs. Winston is an experienced teacher who enjoys the challenge of motivating difficult students and helping them to experience some measure of success.

Some of the other students in the classroom are very active and can be disruptive at times. Generally, however, Mrs. Winston is able to maintain good control due to her strong personality and excellent teaching skills. She is highly organized and utilizes a child-centered curriculum. Recently she has been trying to use cooperative learning techniques but has found this to be difficult due to the make-up of her class. She feels that part of the difficulty stems from the fact that she has more leaders than followers in her class. Many of the leaders are not used to being led by others.

Jimmy, who was normally a leader, was overpowered by the strong personalities of several of the other leaders. Overall, Jimmy's behavior this year has been good. In the past he has not been a significant problem but has had the tendency to be loud and boisterous. Academically, Jimmy is an average student.

Presenting problem: Today seemed to be more stressful than most days. Some of the students arrived at school more agitated than usual. The children seemed to get off task rather easily and it was almost impossible to get them back on track. Several major incidents of arguing took place before lunchtime. Interestingly, Jimmy was not involved in any of the altercations. Jimmy was trying particularly hard to cooperate, hoping that Mrs. Winston would send a good report home to his mother. Mrs. Winston had made a couple of comments about how helpful he was but seemed more interested in the students who were misbehaving.

The afternoon was a repeat of the morning. As the day wore on Mrs. Winston became even more frazzled. Jimmy continued to try to get her attention by being helpful and not getting involved in the fray. However, Mrs. Winston didn't seem to notice. Again, she seemed to be giving all her attention to the misbehaving students.

As the students were lining up at dismissal time, Mrs. Winston put the more rambunctious students at the front of the line and told Jimmy to get at the end of the line. As she stepped into the corridor she heard a commotion in the classroom. "Now what," she thought as she went back into the room. She was not prepared for what she saw. Jimmy was having a temper tantrum like she had never witnessed in all her years of teaching. He was knocking over desks and chairs, ripping down bulletin boards, and dumping the contents of bookshelves onto the floor. All the while he was shouting expletives. Mr. Scanlon, the teacher in the neighboring classroom, rushed to her assistance and physically restrained Jimmy. Mrs. Winston took the other students to the bus while a third teacher called for assistance from the office. Jimmy's mother was called at the hospital and immediately came to the school.

Although Jimmy was physically restrained he continued to shout expletives. Jimmy's anger seemed to be directed at Mrs. Winston. He finally calmed down when his mother arrived at the classroom door. When Jimmy was subdued Mrs. Winston asked him what made him so upset. "You were so helpful all day long. What happened?" she inquired.

Jimmy tearfully responded, "Then why did you send me to the end of the line?"

Questions for discussion and reflection:

1. What are some of the factors that led to Jimmy's explosion? How did his need for positive attention and the fact that he didn't get it lead to his outburst?

2. Why did Mrs. Winston send Jimmy to the end of the line? Why did Jimmy think he was sent to the end of the line? Why was this the final straw?

3. In retrospect, could Jimmy's temper tantrum have been avoided if Mrs. Winston had responded to him differently? What could she have done? Could his actions have been foreseen?

4. Was physical restraint a proper response to Jimmy's out-of-control behavior? What are some guidelines that should be instituted for the use of physical restraint?

5. Knowing that Jimmy is volatile, how should Mrs. Winston handle him in the future? Does this episode indicate that Jimmy has a quick temper or other undiagnosed needs?

6. What does this episode say about Jimmy's leadership skills and his ability to be cooperative? Does he need constant reinforcement?

Chapter 10

Rebellion: The Need for Freedom

Harry Stewart, principal of East High School, had arrived early to prepare for a scheduled suspension hearing. As he was putting the final touches on some of the mandatory paperwork, he began to think of the events that led to the contemplated suspension. The school board had recently instituted a new dress code which had not been well accepted by the students. Several students had written letters to the editor of the school newspaper protesting the new dress code. Stanley Jowell, a student council representative from the junior class had asked Harry to hold an assembly where students could express their views. Thinking that this could be a good lesson in democracy, Harry agreed.

At the assembly yesterday, Stanley made a speech protesting the new dress code that was laced with obscenities. He referred to the school's administration and several teachers as "#%.$# fascists" whose only interest was in limiting students' freedom. He also implied that an assistant principal was a "faggot" and that the school board chairperson wasn't "getting enough at home." Stanley's remarks angered the faculty and caused great embarrassment to the school board chairperson who was present at the assembly, and whose children attended the school. In addition, it took Harry and his staff over 20 minutes to restore order in the auditorium.

Harry didn't quite know what to expect from Stanley's father at the hearing. On the one hand he wondered how any parent would accept such behavior from their child. However, Stanley's father was an attorney known for promoting liberal causes (before entering private practice he had worked for the American Civil Liberties Union). Could he possibly think that Stanley's comments were protected by the First Amendment? Harry just wasn't sure. He was sure, however, that his faculty and the school board chairperson would expect him to take strong disciplinary action. In addition to the suspension he contemplated removing Stanley from the student council and suspending him from the football team. He knew Mr. Jowell would object to the latter action as this would hurt Stanley's chances of getting an athletic scholarship.

As Harry thought about the incident with Stanley, he remembered his own youthful rebelliousness. He had protested the U.S. involvement in Viet Nam while in college and had participated in many anti-war demonstrations and sit-ins. While in high school he had also tested the limits of the dress code. However, this was different. Or was it?

Most of us (especially those of us who grew up in the 60s) can remember the rebelliousness of our youth. We felt a need to express our individuality by refusing to conform to the expectations of "the establishment" in the way we dressed or wore our hair. For the most part our rebellion was harmless enough; however, rebellion can reach an extent that it is either disruptive to the educational process or dangerous.

For purposes of this chapter *rebellion* will refer to actions on the part of students that reach a level of concern for teachers and administrators. Here we are not talking about the student who dyes his hair purple or wears jeans that have more holes than denim. We are not even referring to students who may hold a peaceful demonstration to protest a new school policy. Rather, we are referring to activities engaged in by students that cause a serious disruption to the daily routine or that present a situation that could result in harm to either the rebelling student or others.

Students, particularly those at the high school level, begin to feel a need for freedom. They have reached a point where they require less supervision and are allowed to make more choices for themselves. However, many feel that this is not sufficient and think they are mature enough that they should have complete freedom. When the adults in their lives disagree and attempt to exercise control, the students may rebel. Rebellion can take many forms. It can be symbolic or it can be overt. Students need to learn that rebellion is acceptable as long as the rebellious activities do not infringe on the rights of others. In fact, as the students themselves may point out, our country was founded on rebellion. Indeed, appropriate rebellion is a necessary and welcomed aspect of a democratic society.

Unfortunately, all acts of student rebellion are not appropriate or even in keeping with democratic principles. Rebellious students can, and often do, disrupt classrooms and even entire schools. Disruptive behavior may range from a single student loudly refusing to conform to a classroom teacher's expectations to a large group of students who disrupt a school assembly by shouting obscenities. Student rebellion in symbolic forms can also have an overall disruptive effect. For example, students who wear obscene tee shirts may contend that they are simply exercising their Constitutional right to express themselves; however, such actions can be disruptive to the extent that they draw attention to the wearer and offend others.

Rebellion can, of course, become dangerous when it reaches a level of violence. Unfortunately, those who are rebelling to assert their freedom often disregard the rights of those who may disagree. In their zeal to express themselves, rebellious students may cause property damage or even inflict harm on others. Even if actual harm is not inflicted, the threat of harm crosses the boundaries of acceptable behavior. The rebellious student may also inflict harm on himself or herself. This may happen, for example, when the student uses drugs as a form of rebellion against the mores of society.

Not all rebellion in the classroom is based on social protest. Much rebellion stems from the student's unrealistic desire to exert independence and shed the shackles of authority. This type of rebellion takes the form of pervasive defiance of authority, often for the sake of defiance itself. Rebellious students often do not understand why others are able to exert control over them. They frequently exert their "rights" while disregarding the rights of others. They want freedom but are unable to accept the concept that with freedom comes responsibility.

The task of school officials, of course, is to allow appropriate rebellion while keeping control over actions that can get out of hand. In fact, students can be taught much about democracy by allowing them (and in fact teaching them) to express themselves in appropriate forums. However, as in all aspects of classroom management, limits must be set and those who cross the boundaries of acceptable deportment must be dealt with. A common, effective strategy is to begin by listening to what the rebellious student has to say. Issues should be clarified. If the student's protest is valid, changes should be made. However, when the student's demands cannot, and should not, be met, the student should be given a rational explanation as to why his or her cause for rebellion is unreasonable. This does not mean that the student will accept the explanation or that the explanation will curb the rebellion. There are times when disciplinary sanctions need to be imposed.

Since many of the issues involved with rebellious students are legal and Constitutional issues, the *Additional Reading* section of this chapter includes a supplemental segment that lists court cases involving rebellious students. A reading of these cases will help to clarify the extent to which school officials may limit and control students' rights to express themselves symbolically, orally, and in writing.

Additional Reading

Alley, R. et al. (1990). Student misbehaviors: Which ones really trouble teachers? *Teacher Education Quarterly, 17(3)*, 63–70.

Brendtro, L., and Banbury, J. (1994). Tapping the strengths of oppositional youth: Helping Kevin change. *Journal of Emotional and Behavioral Problems, 3(2)*, 41–45.

Emerson, S., and Syron, Y. (1995). Adolescent satanism: Rebellion masquerading as religion. *Counseling and Values, 39(2)*, 145–159.

Fine, G.A., and Victor, J. (1994). Satanic tourism: Adolescent dabblers and identity work. *Phi Delta Kappan, 76(1)*, 70–72.

Horowitz, H. (1989). The changing student culture: A retrospect. *Educational Record, 70,* 24–29.

Husby, L., and Brendtro, L. (1992). Youth and the city streets. *Journal of Emotional and Behavioral Problems, 1(1),* 46–48.

Lovelace, L. (1995). Exploring writing—from rebellion to participation. *Journal of Learning Disabilities, 28(9),* 554–559.

Shoop, R.J., and Dunklee, D.R. (1992). *School Law for the Principal.* Boston: Allyn & Bacon, Inc.

Timmerman, L. et al. (1989). Augmenting the helping relationship: The use of bibliotherapy. *School Counselor, 36(4),* 293–297.

Victor, S. (1992). Days of their lives: Reflections on adolescent girls and adolescent mothers. *School of Education Review, 4,* 72–81.

Court Cases

Bannister v. Paradis, United States District Court, District of New Hampshire, 316 F. Supp. 185 (1970).

Bethel School District No. 403 v. Fraser, United States Supreme Court, 478 U.S. 675 (1986).

Guzick v. Drebus, United States Court of Appeals, Sixth Circuit, 431 F.2d 594 (1970).

Hazelwood School District v. Kuhlmeier, United States Supreme Court, 484 U.S. 260 (1988).

Jackson v. Dorrier, United States Court of Appeals, Sixth Circuit, 424 F.2d 213, (1970).

Richards v. Thurston, United States Court of Appeals, First Circuit, 424 F.2d 1281 (1970).

Tinker v. Des Moines Independent School District, United States Supreme Court, 393 U.S. 503 (1969).

Trachtman v. Anker, United States Court of Appeals, Second Circuit, 563 F.2d 512 (1978).

Case Study #10-1

Student: Linda

Background: Linda is a 13 year old sixth grader attending a large middle school. Linda lives with her mother. Her 16 year old sister is in the custody of the Department of Youth Services as a result of being a chronic runaway. Her father's whereabouts are unknown and Linda has not had any contact with him in six years. Linda's mother is a cocaine addict, currently in treatment for the third time. In the past 18 months two of her mother's boyfriends have taken their own lives in drug related incidents. Linda has received special education services since grade three to remediate her reading, spelling, and written language skills. Despite this assistance, Linda's reading is only on a third grade level. Her poor reading skills hinder her progress in other subjects. Linda also receives counseling at a local mental health center.

Linda's school history indicates that she has been a behavior problem for several years. She often disregards school rules and defies authority. She has difficulty getting along with her peers, in part because she is quarrelsome. Linda basically does not like being told what to do and will rebel if given an order.

Presenting problem: Linda went to temporarily live with her godmother while her mother is in the drug rehabilitation facility. Her school behavior has worsened since coming to live with her godmother. She is more quarrelsome than ever and has even engaged in fistfights with her peers. She constantly argues with her teachers and other authority figures. Her favorite response to a teacher's request to do something is, "You're not my mother. You can't boss me around." She has been truant on several occasions, has destroyed school property, and has been caught smoking in the girls' restroom. Her fighting and school vandalism have resulted in suspensions. She has been required to make up the missed time when truant and has received numerous detentions for her other acts of misconduct.

Linda's godmother has been very supportive but is at a complete loss as to what to do. She does not have any children of her own and is thus very inexperienced in the parental role. She is looking to the school for some help in managing Linda's behavior. The godmother has cooperated in dealing with Linda's truancy by driving her to school every day and calling the school when Linda is absent. She has also tried to follow through with home sanctions for Linda's school misconduct; however, this has resulted in much stress due to Linda's defiance of the godmother's authority. Linda responds to the godmother's attempts at exercising authority by saying, "I wish you'd leave me alone. I'm old enough to do what I want."

As part of the school's response to Linda's behavior, the school psychologist conducted an evaluation. He found that Linda is very angry and bitter. She feels that no one has the right to "boss" her around and that she should be given more freedom than she has. She thinks school rules are dumb and doesn't understand why she can't have the freedom to take a day off now and then. Linda also thinks that it is unfair that she can't smoke in school. Linda feels that classrooms should have smoking and non-smoking sections just like restaurants. She resents the fact that she must stay with her godmother and doesn't understand why she can't stay by herself in her mother's apartment. "After all I'm old enough to take care of myself," she told the psychologist.

Of greater concern to the psychologist is Linda's lack of affect over the deaths of her mother's boyfriends. Linda was more impressed over the fact that she got to ride in a limo at their funerals. Linda thought that this was "real cool." When asked if she missed the last boyfriend, Linda responded, "Eh, Mom will get another one."

The psychologist feels that Linda herself is a high risk for becoming a substance abuser. It is already known that she smokes and he feels that Linda may have experimented with alcohol and marijuana. He has recommended an in-patient evaluation at a psychiatric facility. Unfortunately, Linda's mother does not have any health insurance due to her present situation and the godmother's insurance does not cover Linda.

Questions for reflection and discussion:

1. Linda feels that only her mother can tell her what to do. To what extent has her mother's absence contributed to her misconduct?
2. What are some of the sources of Linda's anger? What can be done to help her control and appropriately express her anger?
3. Why is Linda rebelling against the authority of her godmother and school officials? What can be done to help Linda realize that a 13 year old girl cannot live on her own and make all her own decisions?
4. Linda's godmother is asking for help. What can the school do to assist her with Linda's behavior? What behavioral intervention strategies can be effectively used in both the home and school?
5. The school psychologist feels that Linda is at high risk for becoming a substance abuser. What signals may be leading him to believe this? Is this due to rebellion or is it environmental? If the psychologist is correct, what can be done to prevent this from happening?
6. Is an in-patient psychiatric evaluation warranted? If so, how can it be paid for?

Case Study #10-2

Student: Keith

Background: Keith is a five year old kindergarten student. He lives with his father and step-mother. His biological parents were never married and his father has had legal custody of him since he was an infant due to his mother's drug usage. When Keith was three years old his biological mother kidnaped him and took him out of the country. It took his father 18 months to find him and bring him home. Keith is an only child although his step-mother is pregnant.

Keith has had no prior experience in either a nursery school or day care center. He has had few opportunities to interact with other children his own age. Keith has, however, shown excellent learning potential. He appears to pick up new concepts quickly and is very curious. He has learned to write his name and has learned to identify most letters and numerals in only a few months.

Socially, however, Keith has had some problems. He does not play well with other kindergarten students and often becomes physical with them. He doesn't like to share with others and will often just take things he wants from other students. For example, one day Keith and another boy, Sean, were working together in the science center. Sean was playing with a dinosaur puppet that Keith wanted. When Sean wouldn't give it to him, Keith took it. When Sean protested, Keith hit him knocking him down. When Keith was disciplined by the teacher he shouted, "You don't like me."

Keith's behavior has been very trying for his teacher. On an almost daily basis he displays some sort of physical aggression toward another student. Conferences with Keith's father have not helped. His father claims that he does not display this behavior at home and plays well with other children in the neighborhood. Keith's father has suggested that the problems Keith has been experiencing may be due to racial bigotry on the part of the other students.

Keith's teacher referred him for a special education evaluation. The evaluation indicated that Keith did not have any learning problems or learning disabilities. However, it did indicate that he had a great deal of pent up anger. He also did not appear to trust adults, especially women. The psychologist suggested that his physical attacks against other students was a way of establishing dominance over them. The evaluation team recommended that Keith finish kindergarten in his current placement, but that he should be transferred to a class for emotionally disturbed students the following year. This recommendation was agreed to by all, including Keith's father.

Presenting problem: Keith's father told him that next year he will be going to another school because he was a "bad boy." Since then Keith has become less physical but more verbally rebellious. During the past few days Keith has refused to conform to classroom rules. He will not obey any of his teacher's commands and defiantly sticks his tongue out at her when told to do something. He responds to reasonable requests with comments such as, "You can't make me do that." He often will do exactly the opposite of what was requested. For example, if told to throw his empty juice box away he will go to the waste basket and take something out of it.

Recently, when asked to put his crayons away, Keith defiantly threw them one at a time to different parts of the classroom. When told to pick all of the crayons up Keith took a box from another student's desk and started to throw those crayons around the room. Exasperated, the teacher called for the principal. The principal took Keith down to her office and sat him at a table. After a few minutes Keith asked, "When are you going to spank me?" The principal explained that she would never spank him even though she was very disappointed in his behavior. Keith put his head on the table and began to cry.

Questions for reflection and discussion:

1. What is the source of Keith's anger? Does his distrust of adults stem from his experience of being kidnaped by his mother?
2. To what extent were Keith's initial behavioral problems related to his not knowing how to get along with and play with other children? What could have been done to teach him more appropriate social skills?
3. Why has Keith become less physical but more rebellious and defiant?
4. Is the class for emotionally disturbed children an appropriate placement? Why or why not? If it is the best placement, is it appropriate to delay it until the start of the next school year?
5. What strategies can Keith's teacher employ to deal with his behavior for the remainder of this school year?

Case Study #10-3

Student: Marty

Background: Marty is a fifth grade student in an elementary school located in a middle class neighborhood. Most of the parents in this neighborhood are blue collar workers. The major employer in the area is an automobile assembly plant. Marty's parents were divorced when he was in the first grade. He lives with his mother and two younger brothers. His father lives in a nearby community and Marty sees him quite frequently. Marty's father has remarried and has one child from his second marriage. Marty's mother is still very bitter about the divorce and resents the fact that his father has remarried.

Marty is a bright student who excels academically when he puts forth appropriate effort. However, he has been a behavior problem since the first grade. He was suspended once in the first grade for fighting. He completed the second and third grades without any major incidents although he was constantly involved in minor incidents. Counseling had been recommended several times but his mother had rejected the idea for various reasons. Unfortunately, however, he was suspended three times during his fourth grade year; twice for fighting and once for ripping the door off a stall in the boys' room. After the last incident his mother finally agreed to counseling.

Marty is very athletic but unfortunately he is also overly competitive to the point that he must win at all costs. He has difficulty with team sports because he gets very angry when his team doesn't win and blames the other players for the team's defeat. When he loses an individual game or his team loses a game, Marty frequently will accuse the opponent of cheating. He was recently ejected from a Youth League football game because he told one of the officials that he was a "stupid idiot" after the official called him for clipping.

Marty's greatest talent, however, is in art. He has won many poster contests and art contests. Mostly, however, he enjoys drawing the villains from comic books. Most of his drawings depict violence or characters sporting weapons. Marty's art talents are so good that his art teacher feels that he could someday become a commercial artist.

Presenting problem: Behaviorally, Marty's fifth grade year has been a disaster. He has reached the point where he rarely will participate in team sports because the other players "stink." He will not engage in individual competition unless he is more than positive that he will win. He is not content to leave other players alone, however. He does his best to interfere with games that are being played during recess on the school playground. For example, if he is able to intercept a stray basketball he will kick it to the far end of the playground. On two occasions he has kicked basketballs onto the school's roof. His art work has taken on a new twist: He likes to draw pictures of buildings, cars, etc. being blown up. He is fascinated with stories in the news of terrorist activities.

In the classroom itself Marty has become more of a nonconformist. His teacher, Mr. Peters, is able to ignore some of his nonconforming behavior because it is relatively harmless. Mr. Peters has taken the attitude that he is going to choose his battles and will confront Marty only when it is absolutely necessary. Mr. Peters is concerned that Marty is accomplishing very little academically. Marty chooses which assignments he wants to complete and will spend his time drawing if he chooses not to do an assignment the rest of the class is working on. Mr. Peters refuses to argue with Marty about whether or not he will complete an assignment; He simply assigns Marty a 0 for every assignment not completed. On his third quarter report card, Marty failed Reading, Math, and Social Studies. For the most part, however, Marty is not disturbing the class.

Mr. Peters is also concerned that Marty often leaves the classroom without permission to go to the boys' restroom or even to wander around the school. When he spoke to Marty about this, Marty responded, "It's a free country, I can go where I want as long as I don't bother anyone." When Mr. Peters tried to explain that he is responsible for Marty and needed to know where he was at all times, Marty emphatically informed him that, "No one is responsible for me."

Mr. Peters decided that Marty should not go on the fifth grade field trip unless one of his parents came along. Mr. Peters was concerned that he would not be able to properly supervise Marty and that it could be dangerous if Marty decided to become uncooperative or decided to leave the group. Marty's mother refused to accompany him on the field trip stating that she didn't think he deserved to go anyway. When Marty was told that he would not be going on the field trip he became enraged and threatened to "blow up the school." When Mr. Peters left school that day he discovered one of his tires had been punctured. Although he could not prove it, he suspected Marty.

Questions for reflection and discussion:

1. Marty has a history of behavior problems. Except for counseling which began in the fourth grade, the only interventions have been disciplinary. What strategies could have been used early in his school career to deal with Marty's behavior?
2. Is Mr. Peters' strategy of "choosing his battles" appropriate? If not, how should he confront Marty's refusal to complete assignments?
3. Is Mr. Peters' concern about what Marty might do on the field trip warranted?
4. Should school officials be concerned about Marty's propensity to draw pictures depicting violent acts? Should they take his threat to blow up the school seriously?
5. Mr. Peters feels that Marty punctured his tire. Given Marty's overall behavioral profile, is it likely that he engaged in retaliatory behavior?
6. What is the prognosis for Marty? What can be done in the future to deal with his rebellious behavior?

Case Study #10-4

Student: Richard

Background: Richard is a 16 year old tenth grader attending a comprehensive high school. He has received special education services since grade three to improve his reading, language, and math skills. Cognitive testing indicates that his I.Q. is in the vicinity of 80. Currently he spends three periods a day in the resource room for academic support. He also sees a school guidance counselor once a week. Richard lives at home with his mother, his step-father, and three half-siblings. Richard is the oldest.

Richard has a history of court involvement since the fifth grade. His transgressions have included shoplifting, breaking and entering, stealing a car, possession of drugs, and trespassing. He spent the summer before grade ten in a Department of Youth Services detention facility. In spite of his extracurricular activities, Richard has not been a major problem in school. He has been involved in some minor altercations with other students and has been suspended on occasion; but basically, he is well liked by his teachers.

Richard's step-father refuses to discipline him because he was once found to be guilty of child abuse after having administered physical punishment to Richard. His mother has little control over him and claims that he won't listen to her.

Presenting problem: Richard started the tenth grade off well. He told his teachers that he had learned his lesson and did not want to return to the DYS facility. However, around mid-year his behavior in school began to deteriorate. He started coming in late, was occasionally truant, and sometimes left the school building in mid-day. Around this time Richard's mother started to call the school one or two mornings a week to see if he was in school. It was later learned that she did this because he had not come home the night before. Richard's teachers reported that he frequently fell asleep in class, especially in his early morning classes. Some teachers felt that he was acting as though he was under the influence of drugs; however, there was no evidence of possession of drugs.

The high school Richard attends has an open campus privilege for juniors and seniors in good standing. This allows them to leave the campus during study halls and other non-class times. When Richard was spoken to by the vice principal about his casual attitude toward school start and dismissal times he pointed to the open campus program and said that it wasn't fair that other kids his same age could come and go as they pleased but he couldn't. He expressed the opinion that it should have nothing to do with the grade a student was in but rather, once a student was 16 the student should have the freedom to make his own decisions. This issue is complicated by the fact that most of Richard's friends are upperclass students who have the open campus privilege.

School officials began to notice that other students were giving things to Richard. At first they gave him portions of their lunch but later this escalated to cigarettes and monetary gifts. School administrators felt that Richard was extorting these gifts but could not get any of the other students to offer any information. Eventually, a parent informed the principal that her son was afraid of Richard and had been threatened with bodily harm if he didn't "pay up." However, the boy was unwilling to speak to the principal for fear of retribution from Richard and his friends. Soon other parents made similar complaints but none of the students were willing to provide any testimony against Richard. The principal wanted to take disciplinary action against Richard but could not gather the necessary evidence to take action.

It has also been learned that Richard was not meeting with his probation officer and had stopped going to court ordered counseling sessions. When his school counselor tried to talk to him about the consequences of these actions, Richard indicated that he really didn't care. He also pointed to the fact that nothing had been done when he stopped meeting with the probation officer. Eventually, he refused to talk to his school counselor saying he wished everyone would "get off my back and leave me alone."

Although Richard continued to attend classes, he did not participate in any class activities, did not work on any assignments, and did not do any homework. He did not bring any materials to class with him and never opened a book. He did not disturb the classes in any way, however. He simply came to class and sat there. This left his teachers feeling quite perplexed. Frankly, they did not understand why he even bothered to come to class.

Since Richard's Individualized Education Plan was due for its annual review, the special education staff decided that a complete reevaluation was warranted. They recognized that his current program was not meeting his needs and that alternatives needed to be investigated. However, Richard refused to cooperate with the school psychologist and the special education teacher was only able to complete half of an achievement test. The portions of the test that were completed indicated that Richard's academic skills were on a third grade level. The principal has suggested that the evaluation and placement team consider transferring Richard to the school district's alternative school. However, the school psychologist feels that Richard finds security at the local high school and that a transfer to an alternative school might cause him to drop out. She feels that as long as he is attending school there is hope.

Questions for reflection and discussion:

1. Richard feels that since he is 16 he should have more freedom. Since he hasn't been given that freedom, he has simply taken it. How can school officials respond to Richard's desire for more freedom at age 16?

2. The school's principal feels that a situation exists that must be addressed. Since he has been unable to gather the evidence needed to suspend Richard, but is receiving parental complaints, he is feeling frustrated. What steps could he take to put an end to the suspected extortion activities?

3. The principal has suggested that an alternative school might be more appropriate for Richard, however, the school psychologist disagrees. What adjustments could be made to Richard's current program so that it would better meet his needs, keep him in school, and forestall a transfer to an alternative school?

4. What should the role of the juvenile court be? How can the school and the court pool resources and work together? What role should Richard's parents play?

5. To what extent is Richard's behavior rebellious and to what extent is it oppositional? Is Richard expressing normal teenage rebellion or has he crossed the line into delinquent behavior?

Case Study #10-5

Student: Trish

Background: Trish is a 16 year old freshman attending a high school in an industrial city that has a high unemployment rate and much poverty. She is in special education classes for four out of five major subjects. She has received special education since third grade.

Trish was born when her mother was only 14 years old. She lives with her mother and two younger brothers in a federal housing project. Trish's mother never married her father and has had no contact with him since Trish was born. Trish's mother did marry the father of her youngest child, but he has since abandoned the family. Mrs. Williams has had several boyfriends who have abused her and the children.

Throughout her schooling Trish has been considered to be a behavior problem. Her behavior has been described as erratic and unpredictable. She often defies and outright challenges authority figures, especially male authority figures. However, at other times she seems to go out of her way to try to please her teachers.

As early as fourth grade Trish showed an unusual interest in boys and was often in the company of older boys. When she was 11 she bragged about having dates with boys who were 15 or 16. The nature of the dates was unknown but she did hang out with an older crowd. Her mother has little control over her and describes her as "wild." She ran away from home at the age of 12 and was found two weeks later in another state.

Trish gave birth to a little girl 15 months ago at the age of 14. At the time Mrs. Williams told the guidance counselor that she thought it was the best thing that could happen to Trish, adding, "I think it will settle her down just like having Trish settled me down." Prior to and immediately after the baby's birth Trish attended the school district's program for teenage mothers. In this program she was taught the importance of proper pre-natal care and was given instruction in child care. However, a few months ago the baby was taken away by the Department of Social Services after the baby's father reported that Trish was using drugs. Trish denied this allegation.

Presenting problem: Trish is pregnant once again. Plans at the present time call for her to finish her freshman year at the high school. During the summer she is to enroll in prenatal care courses designed for young mothers that are offered through a local hospital. The baby is due in September. When Trish is ready to return to school she will enroll in the school district's program for teenage mothers.

School officials are very concerned about Trish. She obviously learned little through her first experience with pregnancy. School counselors have tried to talk to her about her sexual activity and the dangers of engaging in unprotected sex. However, Trish's attitude is that there's no problem in her being pregnant and she seems unconcerned about contracting infectious diseases.

Trish shows little concern about how she will support her offspring. Her mother told school officials, "I'll take care of her and the baby until she's 18, but then she's on her own." Trish's response is, "If I can't work I'll just go on welfare." She adds, "Who knows, I might not even live to be 18."

Trish's lack of concern has spilled over into her academic life. Although she has never been a great scholar, with special education support she has always managed to get by. Since finding out that she is pregnant, Trish has lost interest in school. She comes every day, but puts little effort into her schoolwork. Homework is unheard of. At this point she is failing three of her five major subjects, including two that are taken in the special education program. Teachers report that her failure is due to a lack of effort.

Her behavior has not changed much except that she reacts with more anger and defiance when pressured to perform academically. On one occasion when a teacher was encouraging her to put more effort into her work, Trish told him to "@#$% off!" Just in case he did not hear her, she provided him with a simultaneous sign language interpretation. She has refused to continue her weekly counseling sessions because the counselor "brings up things that are none of her business" and Trish is tired of "people telling me what to do."

School officials feel that their major concern is to help Trish understand the seriousness of her situation. However, Trish has shown little reaction to their attempts in this regard. They are also concerned about her angry outbursts. Although she has always shown disdain for authority figures, she generally has not reacted with anger in the past. She has been known to use mild vulgarities but has never been so colorful or emphatic in her choice of words. School officials are also concerned that after this baby is born, Trish may not return to school. In order to break her current behavioral cycle and provide her with some hope for a better future, school officials want to do everything possible to keep her from dropping out.

Questions for reflection and discussion:

1. What can school officials do to make Trish realize the serious consequences of her actions and the potential danger of continuing on this track?

2. To what extent is Trish's promiscuous behavior indicative of rebellion against authority figures and the expectations of society? To what extent is her behavior environmental?

3. What is the source of Trish's recent anger. What can school officials do to help her deal with it?

4. What strategies can be employed to keep Trish in school and prevent her from dropping out?

5. Is this a hopeless situation or can school officials make a difference? What can they do long-term to change Trish's behavior?

Appendix A

Legal Requirements

General Requirements

Unfortunately, educators' attempts at altering inappropriate student behavior is not always successful. School officials must, from time to time, mete out disciplinary sanctions. In doing so, they must consider legal requirements in addition to what may be most appropriate from an educational or behavioral standpoint. Like it or not, the disciplinary process is a highly legal process. Students today are considered to be full-fledged citizens enjoying the rights and privileges granted by the Constitution, federal laws, and state laws.

Students have not always enjoyed these rights. A few short years ago school officials did not recognize that students had any rights at all. However, in 1967 the U.S. Supreme Court declared that juveniles had constitutional rights in criminal proceedings in its landmark *In re Gault*[1] decision. Two years later constitutional rights were consequently extended to students in the schools in the well-known *Tinker v. Des Moines School District*[2] arm band case. In this decision the Court acknowledged that students did not shed their constitutional rights to freedom of speech or expression at the schoolhouse gate.

Although public school students possess some rights to freedom of speech and expression, they also have some responsibility to act reasonably. School officials retain the right to control student speech if there is a reasonable expectation of disruption. Furthermore, speech that is obscene or offensive can be regulated, especially when the audience is immature.[3] Students also have rights to speech and expression in non-spoken forms, such as the written word, although those rights too can be limited.[4]

---

1. 387 U.S. 1, 87 S. Ct. 1428 (1967).

2. 393 U.S. 503, 89 S. Ct. 733, 21 L. Ed.2d 731 (1969). In this decision the Court held that students had the right to wear black arm bands to school protesting the Vietnam War.

3. *See generally* Bethel Sch. Dist. v. Fraser, 478 U.S. 675, 106 S. Ct. 3159, 92 L. Ed.2d 549 (1986).

4. *See generally* Hazelwood Sch. Dist. v. Kuhlmeier, 484 U.S. 260, 108 S. Ct. 562, 98 L. Ed.2d 592 (1988).

Due process rights are central to the constitutional rights given to juveniles. In a long line of court opinions it has been demonstrated that these rights exist in the schools. The Supreme Court first extended these due process rights to students facing suspension in the *Goss v. Lopez*[5] lawsuit. Here, the Court specifically stated that students facing suspensions of less than 10 days were entitled to informal notice of the charges against them and the opportunity for some sort of a hearing. Furthermore, any student who denies the charge must be told of the evidence against him or her and given the chance to present his or her side of the story. These guidelines are flexible depending on the nature of the misconduct and the severity of the penalty. More formal due process is required for more severe penalties. The Court did not delineate the specific procedures to be followed when an expulsion is the contemplated action, except to say that greater due process would be called for. This increased due process could include a more formal hearing with representation by counsel[6] and cross-examination of witnesses.[7] Although a hearing should be held before a student's removal from school, school officials may hold one after the fact in cases where immediate removal of the student is necessary.

Students With Disabilities

Special requirements exist for disciplining students with disabilities who have an Individualized Education Program (IEP).[8] These requirements are in place to assure that these students are not deprived of their rights to a free appropriate public education under the Individuals with Disabilities Education Act (IDEA),[9] section 504 of the Rehabilitation Act,[10] or the Americans with Disabilities Act (ADA).[11]

Manifestation Decision

Prior to imposing any disciplinary sanction that would result in a change in placement for a student with disabilities, school officials must first deter-

---

5. 419 U.S. 565, 95 S. Ct. 729, 42 L. Ed.2d 725 (1975).

6. Hudgins H.C. and Vacca, R. (1995). *Law and Education: Contemporary Issues and Court Decisions.* Charlottesville, VA: Michie.

7. Shoop, R.J. and Dunklee, D.R. (1992). *School Law for the Principal.* Needham Heights, MA: Allyn & Bacon, 166.

8. For a more thorough treatment of disciplinary requirements when dealing with students with disabilities *see* Osborne, A.G. (1997). *Disciplinary Options for Students with Disabilities.* Dayton, OH: Education Law Association.

9. 20 U.S.C. § 1401 *et seq.*

10. 29 U.S.C. § 794.

11. 42 U.S.C. § 12101 *et seq.*

Index